THE MANDALA Of WISDOM

Everyday Sacred Living
for the Modern Mystic

Julia Anastasiou

Copyright © 2025 Julia Anastasiou
All rights reserved.

No part of this publication may be copied, reproduced, stored in a retrieval system, or transmitted in any form or by any means electronic, mechanical, photocopying, recording, or otherwise without the prior written permission of the author, except for brief quotations used in reviews, articles, or scholarly works.

This book is offered as a companion for personal reflection and spiritual awakening. The practices, insights, and transmissions shared within arise from the author's lived experience, professional training, and intuitive guidance. They are not intended to replace medical, psychological, or therapeutic advice.

Published by Julia Anastasiou
Cover design by Julia Anastasiou
Edited by Carolyn Burdet
ISBN: 9798283797533
First Edition: June 2025
Printed in the United Kingdom

For more information, offerings, and sacred journeys, please visit:
www.juliaanastasiou.com
info@juliaanastasiou.com
@juliaanastasiou108
Podcast: Awakening the Mystic Within

Julia 'Yog Sundari' has walked the path with sincerity and dedication. Her work is not just a book; it is a reflection of her inner journey and commitment to the teachings. I have witnessed her transformation and am pleased to see her share this offering with the world. May it serve as a guide for those seeking balance and truth.

~ **Dr. Yogrishi Vishvketu**, PhD, Founder of Akhanda Yoga Wellbeing

In a world that often feels disconnected from its sacred roots, *The Mandala of Wisdom: Everyday Sacred Living* offers a profound homecoming. Having witnessed firsthand the depth of Julia's expertise and the transformative power of her work, I can say with certainty that this book is far more than a guide—it's a living invitation to reclaim the sacred in our daily lives.

~ **Phoebe Garnsworthy**, best selling author of Daily Rituals

A remarkable, inspiring and outstanding book written by Julia Anastasiou, a gifted yogini, mystic, medicine woman and teacher, who weaves together her profound wisdom with a rich tapestry of living practices - clearly explained, grounded in experience, and applicable to everyday life. Every page radiates Julia's authentic journey toward oneness and wholeness, reflecting her deep connection and alignment to the rhythms of the Earth and the cosmos. Her ability to distil that sacred journey, which she has undertaken by herself and, through her teachings, with many women world-wide, into a sacred wisdom path that we can follow and make our own, is indeed a rare gift to the reader.

This book is a 'must read'. It is a powerful guide for everybody who wants to bring the transformative power of the sacred into their life, nourish their soul, align with their deeper purpose and create a life imbued with sacred meaning.

~ **Christa Mackinnon** (MSc); psychologist & shamanic teacher; Hay House author; founder of Bridging the Worlds & Modern Medicine Woman Training School

DEDICATION

To my beloved family, my husband and boys, thank you for walking beside me with love, patience, and grace. You have supported my unfolding, engaged with my journey, and given me the space to grow, to root, and to bloom. This work rests upon the foundation of your unwavering love.

To my mum, thank you for your constant love, support, and the quiet encouragement that has always held me. To my dad, though you have passed beyond this realm, your spirit walks with me still. May this offering honour your memory.

To the courageous souls who seek wisdom and transformation, may these pages be a lantern on your path, guiding you ever closer to your sacred truth and to the divine wisdom that already lives within you.

To the divine Spiral of Wisdom Keepers, the women who have gathered in circle, walked beside me on retreat, and danced through the seasons, your devotion, your courage, and your presence have breathed life into this sacred journey.

To the Divine Feminine and Sacred Masculine, to the Earth below and the Cosmos above, thank you for holding me in your great rhythm, for whispering ancient truths through wind, fire, waters, and stars.

And to my friends, teachers, mentors, and the wise women who have illuminated my path with love and insight, this book carries the imprint of your sacred transmissions.

ENTERING THE MANDALA:
A PATHWAY TO SACRED LIVING

Dear One,
You who hold this book in your hands,
You who have heard the whisper —
soft as rose petals, fierce as firelight —
this is your calling.

You are not here by chance.
You have entered the mandala.
This circle, this spiral, this path of remembrance
has been turning through your bones long before now.

Take a breath.
Feel the earth beneath you,
the sky above you,
the ancient ones around you.

There comes a time when the whisper of the soul
grows louder than the noise of the world.
When we begin to yearn
not just for answers, but for meaning.
Not just for routine, but for rhythm.
Not just for doing, but for being —
for beauty, purpose, and devotion.
This book is a remembering.
A return to the ancient knowing
that everything can be sacred

when we walk through life as ceremony.

You are invited now
to walk barefoot through these pages.
To awaken what has long slept.
To reclaim what was never truly lost.
To remember the sacred that lives within you.

You'll find rituals and reflections,
seasonal wisdom, elemental practices,
ancestral stories and personal thresholds.
Each chapter is a petal on the mandala of sacred living —
an invitation to step deeper into yourself and into the Great Mystery.

This is not a book to rush.
It is a companion. A candle. A compass.
Read it with presence.
Let it be a conversation, a ceremony, a caress.

And if you come across symbols, archetypes or ancient language
that stir something unnamed within you,
know you are not alone.

A Glossary: A Language of the Sacred awaits at the back of this book should you wish to explore deeper meaning and resonance.

As you cross this threshold,
may your heart open like a flower at first light.
May your soul rise like mist from the land of Avalon.
And may the wisdom you meet here
be not new, but deeply known —

etched in your breath, your blood, your remembering.

This is not just a book to be read.
It is a temple to be entered.
A circle to be walked.
A flame to be tended.

May it bless you.
May it change you.
May it bring you home.

With love,
Julia

TABLE OF CONTENTS

Dedication i
Entering the Mandala: A Pathway to Sacred Living iii
Table of Contents vii
The Mandala of Wisdom 1
PART I Foundations of Sacred Living 15
    Chapter 1 Moving from Mundane to Daily Sacred 17
    Chapter 2 Creating an Altar: Sanctuary for the Soul 27
    Chapter 3 Gathering: The Art of Holding Circle 34
    Chapter 4 Holding Safe Space in a Sacred Circle 42
    Chapter 5 Opening Ritual: The Call to Sacred Living 52
    Chapter 6 Smudging: A Smoke Ritual for Creating Sacred Space. 64
    Chapter 7 Treasures for the Altar 72
    Chapter 8 Embracing the Elements 84
    Chapter 9 The Mandala as a Portal 92
PART II Walking the Wheel 108
    Chapter 10 Mandala Directions: Your Inner Compass 110
    Chapter 11 East: New Beginnings 117
    Chapter 12 South: Passion and Transformation 121
    Chapter 13 West: Harvest and Reflection 125
    Chapter 14 North: Reflection and Renewal 129
    Chapter 15 Ether: Great Spirit Connecting As Above, So Below .. 133
PART III Embodying the Mystic Within 139
    Chapter 16 The Power of Invocation 141
    Chapter 17 Invocations for Sacred Ceremony 149

Chapter 18 The Divine Feminine and Sacred Masculine 155
Chapter 19 The Hero's Journey and Shero's Journey 163
Chapter 20 Embracing Shadow: Sacred Journey of Inner Growth 175
Chapter 21 The Wheel of the Year: Sabbats and Solstices 189
Chapter 22 Moon Cycles: Reflection and Manifestation 201
Chapter 23 Sacred Mandala Integration and Reflection 229

Final Blessing A Closing for the Journey 235
Glossary of Sacred Terms A Language of the Soul 237
Epilogue The Spiral Continues 246
Acknowledgements 248
About the Author 250
Connect with Julia Anastasiou 252

THE MANDALA OF WISDOM

INTRODUCTION:
FROM ASHRAM TO YOGINI IN THE YURT

The Mandala of Wisdom is a culmination of my own journey. Over thirty years ago, I began working as a holistic therapist, healer, teacher and soul guide. In 2020, I was at a yoga ashram in India, teaching on an advanced yoga teacher training, as the world went into lockdown. After months of being away from home, I was sent back to the UK and the world as I knew it shifted. Everything changed.

I'd been running a full program of yoga classes, workshops, courses and retreats, as a moment's pause in London's busy life. Now nobody could go to yoga class, nobody could meet up. My life coaching clients, my yoga students and the circle of women who had come on retreats with me, were eager to continue to connect to the energy of our circle, and I felt a pull to create a space to find a way for us to gather once more.

So, I lovingly redesigned our Mongolian yurt nestled in the back garden of our London home. Once alive with rituals, drumming, and in-person teachings, the space had rested while I was away on teaching in India. During the stillness of lockdown, I returned to it sweeping the floor, lighting candles, and weaving in new intentions. What emerged was more than a return; it was a rebirth.

INTRODUCTION

The online platform I created within those sacred canvas walls became a global sanctuary a place where women from all over the world could gather in ceremony, ritual, and deep soul healing.

The land where the yurt is situated is near a Neolithic tumulus in Shooter's Hill, Greenwich. I could feel the presence of the ancestors of this land guiding every class, every workshop, and sacred circle. The earth beneath me provided unwavering support, and the cosmos above me infused each moment with divine inspiration.

It was here in this sacred space in my own back yard that I began to weave together the teachings of the Yogini, the Shamanka, and the Urban Priestess.

This period of initiation, as I reflect on it now, marked the beginning of a new phase in my spiritual practice, one that transcended physical boundaries. The yurt, which was my base for classes, ceremony and circles for the next three years, was too cold for teaching during the winter months, so I retreated inside to my indoor therapy room as the energy drew deeper inside us for winter.

Yet the essence of that sacred space and the energy of the ancestors, continued to guide me, and our circle of women across the world, on our own journey, as our practice deepened to hold ceremonies to heal our ancestral lines, sustained by a growing and reverent connection.

As the days became warmer, I extended the energy of the yurt into the garden. I planted raised beds, weaving herbs, flowers and nature into my daily rituals, as the sun rose in the east, and appeared to turn southwards in the sky, before setting in the west. Even when we were unable to travel, we could do our sun salutations while turning to face the sun on its journey, bowing to the directions, as the calendar turned through the seasons, completing the wheel of the year. At the heart of the space, I placed a circle of stone slabs that would serve as an anchor for our sacred medicine wheel.

The Mandala of Wisdom is the culmination of this integration of rituals honouring the cycles of nature. Through the creation of sacred space for yoga, meditation, ceremony and Celtic shamanic rituals of our ancient land, I have woven these ancient practices together, adapting them to meet the needs of our modern world to include everyday ways of integrating the experiences.

The work that began as a circle of connection in that small space at a time when gathering in person and travelling far from home was restricted, now reaches far and wide in a circle joined by wisdom seekers from around the world. Our morning classes continue to grow online going deeper into the sacred journey. I am honoured to have held ceremony to honour the ancestors and to heal the mothers and fathers of our ancestral lineage.

As the world opened, I have now opened ***The Mystery School of The Mystic: The Path of the Rose.*** This mystery school is a sacred portal that allows us to connect as an online community and gather for residential retreats and sacred pilgrimage journeys together.

In a world that often rushes forward, disconnected from its roots and the sacred rhythms of life, there is a call for some deeper knowing, a deep, resonant summons to return to a more profound way of being. This work with the community of women who have joined me on our journey into everyday sacred, continues to deepen, reminding me of the powerful wisdom that flows when we align with the rhythms of the earth and the cosmos.

Introduction

The Mandala of Wisdom: Everyday Sacred Living for the Modern Mystic is an invitation to embark on this journey of homecoming, guided by archetypes that represent the Divine aspects of life: Yogini, Mystic, Visionary, Shamanic Medicine Woman, Urban Priestess, and Luminary. Each of these roles embodies a facet of a holistic, sacred life, living practices that are as ancient to the landscape as they are relevant in our modern world.

The work is not just mine it belongs to the growing community of women who have joined me on this journey, who have walked this path with me, forming a Spiral of Wisdom Keepers. Month after month, these women joined me online when we were not able to meet in person, reuniting when the world's horizons opened again, and I am forever grateful for their participation in this journey. Even when we could not meet under the same roof, we have gathered in the sacred space, and this energetic space is a tangible connection we share. We have formed a community that supports and uplifts one another.

With deep gratitude, I offer this work as a companion for your own journey of sacred living.

May it be a blessing on your path.
May it bring you home to the sacred in the everyday.
May you remember you were never alone.

WHISPERS FROM THE SPIRAL: VOICES OF THE MANDALA

Before this book begins, I offer you these voices. Not as proof, but as presence. Not as praise, but as a sacred weaving lives that have moved through the spiral and been moved in return. Each word shared here is a thread in the living Mandala, a reflection of what becomes possible when we remember the sacred in the everyday.

This section is a gift from Spirit, it arrived as a clear and unwavering message.

"Let their voices be heard first."

There was no doubt. It was as if the Mandala itself began to speak asking that the lived experiences, the real transformations, and the quiet remembrances of those who have walked this spiral be honoured here, at the very beginning. Not as testimonials, but as transmissions.

And so, I listened.

These words come from women across the world who have walked beside me in circle, in stillness, and in ceremony. They have danced with the elements, prayed with the Earth, and remembered their own rhythm. What they share here is not just gratitude it is soul truth. It is embodiment. It is what happens when we gather in devotion and walk the spiral path together.

Introduction

Beloved Mystic,
May you feel the echo of your own story within theirs. May these reflections meet you where you are and open a doorway into the mystery that awaits. You are not alone on this path. You are already part of the circle... Blessed Be.

"The Mandala of Wisdom has been a guiding light throughout the last five years a sacred container that brought consistency, depth, and soul to my daily practice. Each spiral has carried its own energy, its own medicine, helping me reconnect with the Divine Feminine and remember who I truly am. Being held in this space by Julia's intuition and presence has allowed me to receive powerful insights and feel genuinely seen. The mandala became more than a structure it became a living embodiment of devotion, transformation, and sisterhood. I am deeply grateful for this path and for the unwavering circle of women who continue to rise together each day."

~ Jackie, Swansea, Wales

"Sitting in circle each morning has become the foundation of my day. It is something much deeper than yoga and meditation - it is the ritual, the connection, the heart opening - allowing the flow of the Divine Feminine to weaver her way through us and reveal the ancient wisdom encoded within us."

~ Lucy, Kent, UK

"The Mandala of Wisdom is a sacred rhythm in my life a daily practice of remembering who I am at a soul level. It's not just an embodiment practice; it is a return to gnosis. Each morning, it brings me back to the still point within the wonder, the knowing, the mystery. It nourishes my soul and meets me exactly where I am, just as it does for every woman in the circle. This is a priceless practice a living, breathing mandala I am deeply grateful and honoured to be part of."

~ Gillian, Cork, Ireland

"Each morning as I lay down my mat, I do so with serenity, peace, and a quiet sense of joy — welcoming a sacred practice I choose again and again. As I light my candle and join my fellow *Mandala Spiralists* to the sound of the heart, I know I've come home.

Morning Spirals with Julia have been a lifeline — especially during the pandemic. This practice has not only held me but shaped me. It grounds and uplifts my days, weeks, and seasons. Here, my beliefs are honoured. I'm free to express my truth, held in a circle of light where the foundation — Julia — is loving, mystical, strong, and deeply real. This is more than a practice. It's a path of remembrance. A love letter not only to Julia but to myself, as her teachings invite me to dive deeper into my own heart, to experience healing, self-love, and expansion. We walk together, yet each on our own unique journey — guided by intuition, held in sisterhood. On hard days, we are carried. On joyful days, we are celebrated. Even in the everyday, this circle is a light in my life.

With deep gratitude, let these words be a prayer of appreciation — to Julia, to the women, to *The Mandala of Wisdom*. A sacred vortex of rose light, ancient teachings, joy, tears, and laughter — forever blooming in my heart."

~ Anette Lindquist, Sweden.

"The Mandala of Wisdom has compassionately guided me to weave a cocoon of mindful presence and inner stillness. Julia's teachings continue to hold me with grace — nourishing, healing, inspiring, and awakening me along the path of growth and transformation."

~ Melissa, Alentejo, Portugal

"Being part of The Mandala of Wisdom has opened my heart to

Introduction

trust and cultivate love for myself. I remember my vow to see beauty in everyone and everywhere. Julia's wisdom runs deep and I am so inspired by her."

~ Karen, New York, USA

"I came to the Mandala at a time when I had forgotten how to trust my own inner voice. Through these spirals, I've not only reconnected to my intuition, but also rediscovered joy in the simple sacredness of life. The breath, the movement, the rhythm of it all it's a homecoming I didn't know I was seeking."

~ Emma, London, UK

"Our morning spirals have become the sacred ground upon which I root each day. Over time, this space has woven a tapestry of deep connection to myself, too Julia, and to the radiant circle of women who now feel like soul family. With each practice, I soften, expand, and open to new inner landscapes. I feel held, guided, and profoundly grateful. It's as though I've arrived not just in the right place, but in the right rhythm of being."

~ Francesca, Italy

"If you feel deeply that there is so much more magic to life, then this is where you will find it. I did!"

~ Kim, Cyprus

"Walking the spiral with you has awakened a deeper remembering in my soul one that speaks in the language of stillness, symbols, and sacred rhythm. Your teachings have been both anchor and compass, guiding me gently back to my own truth. With deep gratitude, I honour the way your wisdom continues to ripple through my everyday life."

~ WendieSue, Texas, USA

"Working with Julia has opened the doorway to the most authentic expression of myself a sacred remembering of who I truly am and what I'm here to do. Through every class, coaching session, journey and healing space, I've been given the tools to transform, to soften, to rise. The Mandala of Wisdom has been a vital part of that unfolding weaving presence, purpose and embodiment into my daily life. I am forever grateful for the depth, the devotion, and the light Julia brings to this path."

~ Marie Louise, Pennsylvania, USA

"I joined the spiral in early 2023, drawn in by a dear friend who knew Julia's sacred, vibrant, and inclusive way of teaching would speak to my soul. From the beginning, I was captivated by the way Julia 'breaks the rules' blending ancient feminine wisdom with the timeless practices of yoga, all held within a container of honesty, vulnerability and grace. Despite the distance between hemispheres, this daily practice has become a powerful source of nourishment, anchoring me through life's challenges. My mind is steadier, my body more supple, and my heart deeply grateful. In this circle of women, transformation unfolds and together, we ripple peace, love, and wisdom into the world. That is the true gift of The Mandala of Wisdom."

~ Amanda, Australia

"Thank you for what you do. My life is so much better for being part of this circle. The synchronicity of the mandala always amazes me just what I need to hear often comes through in class, as an answer to a question I didn't know I was asking. It fills me with a profound sense of connection and grounds me."

~ Anne, Portland, Oregon, USA

INTRODUCTION

"Working with Julia through The Mandala of Wisdom has been profoundly transformative. Julia's teachings come straight from the heart authentic, unique, and deeply rooted in truth. Each morning spiral is a space where I feel safe to be vulnerable, supported in my growth, and inspired by the wisdom shared. The mandala is a daily touchstone of connection, community, and inner alignment. I feel so grateful to begin my days in this way."

~ Faye, Portsmouth, England

"Since joining the morning spirals in April 2020, The Mandala of Wisdom has become an anchoring force in my life a space of stability, flow, and daily renewal. Through Julia's intuitive guidance and generous heart, this sacred container has nurtured a rhythm of movement, breath, meditation, music and inner reflection that continues to nourish my soul. It is the first time I have truly sustained such a consistent and meaningful practice, and it has transformed my relationship with myself and my day. The wisdom woven through each spiral the rituals, the repetition, the gentle evolution has helped me connect more deeply to my own inner knowing. Julia's presence is a radiant light in this circle, and I am endlessly grateful for the love she pours into this community. I offer this reflection in memory of my dear friend Laura, whose encouragement brought me here may her spirit continue to spiral with us."

~ Helen, London, UK

"I have been journeying with Julia since 2016, and throughout the years, I've continually marvelled at her intuitive ability to sense what I need often before I even speak it aloud. Her guidance has helped me uncover deep truths about myself and, more importantly, to embrace and navigate life on my own terms.

terms. Working with Julia feels like gently peeling back the layers of an onion each one revealing more of who I truly am. She has created a safe harbour where I feel seen, held, and free to explore. It's hard to put into words the depth of transformation I've experienced through our work together. Julia has opened a new way of seeing myself and my life a more grounded, empowered, and expansive perspective. Within me, she has helped cultivate "a mandala of wisdom," a sacred space of clarity, acceptance, and growth. I am endlessly grateful for all the ways she has supported and guided us."

~ Gael, Devon, UK

"The Mandala of Wisdom has been a lifeline and a lighthouse. In the most tender, uncertain seasons of my life, this daily practice became my anchor gently guiding me back to myself. Julia creates a space where I feel completely held, where tears are welcomed, and where I remember that I am sacred, too. The spiral has become a part of who I am."

~ Andrea, London, UK

"There is a rare kind of medicine in this work. In The Mandala of Wisdom, I found a space where I could exhale fully and feel seen not for what I do, but for who I am becoming. Julia's presence is like a soft drumbeat in the dark, reminding me of the path when I forget. I feel braver, softer, and more whole."

~ Laura, London, UK

"This circle has been an initiation into sisterhood, into embodiment, and into truth. The Mandala isn't just something I attend; it's something I live. The rituals have found their way into my mornings, my relationships, even how I listen to myself. It's changed everything quietly and profoundly."

~ Mandy, London, UK

Introduction

Being part of The Mandala of Wisdom has brought me both clarity and a deep sense of belonging. Over a decade ago, I joined Julia's weekly yoga class a practice she has lovingly refined into a feminine flow enriched with breathwork, deep relaxation, and the healing resonance of the gong. The annual yoga retreat has become a sacred rhythm in my year. Julia creates such a nourishing space, guiding each woman on a meaningful journey. She shares her wisdom so generously from yoga and meditation to ancestral healing and beyond. I feel truly blessed and deeply grateful."

~ Lee, London, UK

"I met Julia through a meditation group and was immediately drawn to her work with women and energy. She gently guided me to release long-held patterns of negative thinking, helping me move forward with greater clarity and a renewed sense of positivity. One of the most profound experiences was being part of a women's circle on ancestral maternal healing. Through that sacred container, I reconnected with my late mother's love not just her memory, but the gifts she passed on. Julia's compassionate guidance, along with the sisterhood she so beautifully holds, gave me a deeper understanding of my roots and how to honour that legacy through my own daughters."

~ Vittoria, California, USA

"Julia's wisdom and gentle, meditative leadership have transported me beyond the everyday world. Through her guidance, I've connected with ancient spirit and the wisdom of the ages awakening a deeper, broader perspective on life. This has allowed me to approach daily matters with more grace and presence, serving my family and community with a natural wisdom birthed from Julia's incredible insights and sacred holding."

~ Lyn, London, UK

"The Wise Women Spiral is one of the most precious gifts I've ever received, a sanctuary of female empowerment, spiritual connection, and deep community. For over three years now, I've been part of this sacred circle, and my heart is full of gratitude. Under Julia's gentle, wise, and inspirational guidance, profound connection has blossomed. My life has truly transformed. Each morning now has structure and meaning. I no longer feel isolated, because I know I'll meet the circle online — a touchstone of presence and purpose. At a time when many women feel lost or alone, this space has supported me to embrace my Wise Woman phase with pride and power.

I feel more spiritually connected than ever. My intuition is alive. My soul feels known. And I've made brave, life-changing decisions that have brought me the freedom and liberation I had longed for.

Julia is a gift from the universe. The Spiral she has created is a living transmission of love — sacred, grounded, and beautifully curated to reflect exactly what we need. Every week, I learn something new, in self-care, in spirit, in soul. Her love flows through every word, every moment, and through each of us."

~ Suzie, Gloucestershire, UK

PART I
FOUNDATIONS OF SACRED LIVING

Chapter 1
Moving from Mundane to Daily Sacred

Every morning, as the first light of dawn stretches across the sky, I enter ceremony. Guiding a morning ritual in my yurt, leading a global gathering online, or simply placing my feet upon the earth in silent reverence, the ritual begins the moment I wake. There is no separation between the sacred and the ordinary; my breath is the invocation, my movement is the prayer, my body is the altar. Each day is a sacred dance, one of presence, devotion, and remembrance.

For years, I sought the sacred in distant lands, in temples, on mountaintops, beneath waterfalls, and within the great stone circles of our ancestors. But what I have come to understand is this: Ceremony is not something we enter. It is something we become.

The body is the temple.
The breath is the offering.
The practice is the ritual.
And life itself is the ceremony.

There was a time in my life when the days felt like a whirlwind a blur of demands, responsibilities, and distractions, that left me disconnected and ungrounded. It was in this season that I discovered the power of ritual. By setting aside even the simplest moments lighting a candle, whispering a prayer, or breathing deeply, I found an anchor in the chaos.

Rituals became a lifeline, a return to the sacred essence of life.

There's a transformative power to bringing the sacred into our life with daily rituals. When we engage in rituals with intention and mindfulness, we invite the divine into our daily lives, creating a bridge between the mundane and the mystical. Rituals are the threads that weave the fabric of our spiritual lives. They ground us, guide us through life's storms, and connect us to the sacred. In a world that often pulls us in many directions, rituals offer a return a moment of stillness, a recalibration of soul.

In The Mandala of Wisdom: Everyday Sacred Living, daily rituals form the threads that weave intentionality, mindfulness, and connection into the fabric of our lives. These simple rituals hold the profound potential to transform our existence, grounding us in the present moment and aligning us with our deeper purpose.

By integrating meaningful rituals into our daily routine, we create a sacred space where the mundane becomes extraordinary, and every action is imbued with spiritual significance.

THE ESSENCE OF RITUALS

Rituals are deliberate actions performed with intention and awareness. Unlike habits, which are often unconscious repetitions, rituals are conscious practices that engage the body, mind, and spirit. They offer structure and sanctuary amidst the chaos. Rituals are moments of pause where we reconnect with ourselves, honour our intentions, and align with the divine.

This awareness crystallised in me not in a grand temple, but in the quiet sanctity of daily practice where a simple inhale becomes a holy act, and a virtual morning circle holds the same sacredness as a fire lit ceremony beneath the stars.

MOVING FROM THE MUNDANE TO THE SACRED

Rituals invite us to transform the ordinary into the extraordinary. By approaching even the simplest actions with intention, we infuse life with sacred energy, creating moments of connection and meaning.

Ask yourself: *Where do you feel rushed or disconnected? What could become sacred, if given the chance?*

THE TRANSFORMATIVE POWER OF DAILY RITUALS

Understanding the profound benefits that daily rituals offer can motivate us to create and maintain sacred practices. Here are just some of the transformative effects:

- **Grounding and Stability:** Rituals anchor us in the present moment, providing stability during uncertain times. They establish a rhythm, creating a predictable pattern that brings peace and security.
- **Mindfulness and Presence:** Engaging in rituals requires full presence, cultivating mindfulness and deepening our awareness of thoughts, feelings, and surroundings.
- **Intentional Living:** Rituals infuse life with intention, transforming ordinary moments into acts of meaning and purpose.
- **Connection to the Sacred:** Rituals create a bridge to the divine, reminding us of the sacredness of life, the interconnectedness with all that exists.
- **Personal Empowerment:** Through rituals, we reclaim

control over our narrative, empowering ourselves to shape our reality and honour our self worth.

WHAT IS A MANDALA?

The Mandala of Wisdom began as a lived experience—within the circular walls of a Mongolian yurt in my London garden. As I swept its floor and relit its altar during lockdown, something ancient stirred. That circle became a teacher, a container, a compass. From its sacred centre, our global gatherings spiralled outward—first as daily rituals, then as seasons of transformation, eventually forming a living mandala of remembrance. What began as a circle of connection became a spiral of awakening.

A mandala, in its essence, is a sacred symbol found across spiritual traditions. Derived from the Sanskrit word for 'circle,' a mandala represents wholeness, unity, and the infinite nature of existence. It is both a visual motif and an energetic map—a reflection of the cosmos, of nature's rhythms, and of the sacred architecture within our own soul. Traditionally used in meditation and ritual, the mandala offers a portal into deeper awareness. Its form mirrors the cycles of life, the turning of the seasons, and the spiralling journey of personal and collective evolution. Each part contains the whole.

In *The Mandala of Wisdom*, this ancient symbol is not merely illustrated—it is embodied. Each ritual, each breath, each sacred pause becomes a petal in the unfolding pattern of your life. Through conscious and devotional action, we spiral inwards towards essence and outwards toward service. Just as no two mandalas are the same, your sacred path is utterly unique. You are the weaver of this mandala. Your life is the canvas. And ritual is the golden thread that brings your soul's essence into form.

CRAFTING YOUR DAILY RITUALS

Creating meaningful daily rituals involves reflection, intention, and creativity. Here are some steps to guide you in crafting rituals that resonate with your unique path and awaken the divine feminine within:

- **Reflect on Your Needs and Intentions:** Consider what you need in your life right now. Are you seeking grounding, clarity, peace, or inspiration? Reflect on your intentions and what you hope to achieve or cultivate through your rituals.
- **Honour the Cycles:** The divine feminine is closely connected to the cycles of nature. Incorporate elements honouring these cycles, such as moon phases, seasonal changes, and personal rhythms. Aligning your rituals with these natural cycles enhances your connection to divine feminine energy.
- **Engage the Senses:** To deepen your connection to the ritual, incorporate elements that engage your senses. Light a candle, burn incense, play soothing music, or use essential oils. These sensory elements can enhance the experience and anchor you in the present moment.
- **Be Consistent:** Consistency is key to the influence of rituals. Choose a time of day that works best for you and commit to your ritual practice. Whether it's in the morning, afternoon, evening, or at nighttime, repeating the ritual with regularity will help embed the ritual into your daily life.
- **Infuse with Intention:** Whatever your ritual involves, perform it with clear intention. Focus on the purpose of the ritual and what you hope to achieve. Visualise your intentions manifesting and feel the emotions associated with them.

Daily Rhythm Rituals

- **Morning Ritual:** Begin your day with gratitude. Light a candle, take a few deep breaths, and set an intention for the day. Spend a few minutes meditating or journaling to align with your goals.
- **Midday Ritual:** Take a break to reconnect with nature. Step outside, feel the sun on your skin, and breathe deeply. Reflect on your progress and recalibrate if necessary.
- **Evening Ritual:** Transition into rest with a calming ritual. Dim the lights, play soothing music, and write three things you're grateful for in a journal. Meditate or practice gentle stretching to release the day's tension.

Awakening The Divine Feminine Through Rituals

At the heart of many rituals lies the symbology and connection to the divine feminine. The divine feminine embodies nurturing, intuition, creativity, and the cyclical nature of life. By awakening this energy within us, we honour the sacredness of all life and tap into the profound wisdom inherent in the feminine aspects of our being.

The divine feminine is a source of deep inner knowing, compassion, and receptivity. Incorporating rituals that awaken this energy allows us to align with the universal flow of creation and intuition, cultivating a balanced and harmonious existence. These rituals remind us of the importance of nurturing ourselves and others, listening to our inner voice, and embracing the natural cycles of growth, rest, and renewal.

To awaken the divine feminine within, consider rituals that celebrate nurturing, creativity, and intuition:

- **Moon Rituals:** Align your intentions with the moon's phases. Set goals during the new moon and release what no longer serves you during the full moon.
- **Goddess Invocation:** Light a candle and call upon a goddess whose energy resonates with your journey. Ask for her wisdom and guidance.
- **Creative Expression:** Dedicate time to creative practices like painting, writing, or dancing, make your expression the ritual. Let your body speak.

Affirmation
I honour the sacred rhythm of my life.
Through daily rituals, I awaken the divine within.
I embrace the present moment, and live with purpose, meaning, and intention.

CONSCIOUS YOGA FLOW AND PRANAYAMA

Engage in yoga flow, moving mindfully through poses that support and embody your intention. Let your breath guide your movements, creating a harmonious dance between body and spirit. As your body flows through the postures, notice the emotions and thoughts that arise, acknowledging them without judgement and releasing them into the rhythm of your practice. Each posture becomes a prayer, each breath an invocation of the sacred. Incorporate pranayama yogic breathing practice to deepen your connection and focus and a profound sense of presence to your practice.

Meditation

After your yoga flow, settle into meditation. Find a comfortable seated position, close your eyes, and turn your awareness inward. Focus on your breath, a mantra, or simply the stillness within. Allow your mind to quieten, your heart to open, and your spirit to soar.

Meditation is the gateway to deeper wisdom, inner peace, and divine connection. In this sacred space of stillness, you can commune with your higher self, receive insights, and experience profound healing. Let this time be a return to your true essence, a moment of deep alignment with the sacred within and around you.

Your Prayer or Invocation

With your intention set, speak a prayer or invocation. This can be a traditional prayer from your spiritual path, a personal invocation crafted from the depths of your heart, or even a simple, sincere plea for guidance and support. The act of speaking out loud infuses your words with vibrational power, aligning your intention with universal energies.

Drinking Your Elixir

Prepare and drink an elixir a sacred beverage that nourishes and supports your practice. This could be cacao, herbal tea, infused water, or any drink that aligns with your intention. As you prepare this sacred drink, infuse it with your intention. Imagine its ingredients carrying the energy of your goals into your body, offering both physical sustenance and spiritual alignment.

Consider what will be supportive to your well being. Chamomile is a herbal tea to bring calm, mint enhances clarity, and ginger is stimulating to the sense and helps to ground you in your body. Allow this elixir to embody your intention physically, fortifying your body and spirit for the journey ahead.

PULLING AN ORACLE CARD

Pulling an oracle card as part of your practice brings divine insight and guidance. If a message arises that feels particularly profound, it can be helpful to journal about it to help you integrate its wisdom fully into your awareness. Shuffle the cards with an open heart and mind and select one intuitively. The message on the card often provides guidance, confirmation, or new perspectives on your path.

Reflect on the card's imagery and message. How does it relate to your intention? What wisdom does it offer? Allow this guidance to permeate your consciousness, enriching your practice with insights and deepening your connection to the divine.

As you close your practice, remember that each movement, each breath, each moment of stillness is a part of the Mandala. It is a thread in the great web of existence, linking you to the past, the present, and the unfolding mystery of the future. Just as the dawn returns each morning, just as the moon waxes and wanes, the wisdom of the Mandala is always present, waiting to be remembered and embodied.

Chapter 2
Creating an Altar: Sanctuary for the Soul

One morning, as the soft light of dawn stretched across my space, I gathered fresh primroses, their pale yellow petals carrying the promise of spring, and placed them beside a small bowl of water, reflecting the gentle light. As I arranged these offerings with care and placed them on a little table which serves as an altar, I felt an inexplicable sense of harmony settle within me.

I remember creating my first altar during a time when life felt chaotic and overwhelming. With a few simple objects a candle, a rose quartz crystal, and a handwritten intention I carved out a space of stillness amidst the noise. That small corner of my home became a sanctuary, a place where I could reconnect with myself and the divine. It taught me that an altar need not be elaborate; it simply needs to hold meaning, presence, and intention.

An altar is more than just a collection of objects; it is a mirror of your soul, reflecting the light of your intentions, the depth of your prayers, and the vastness of your spiritual aspirations. It is where the sacred meets the ordinary, transforming your daily rituals into acts of reverence and devotion, inspiring deeper connection to self and spirit. The altar is a space to pause, breathe, and connect with the divine essence that flows through all things.

One autumn day, as I wandered through an ancient grove, the scent of earth and moss thick in the air, I traced my fingers along the ridges of a weathered stone on the ground. I knew it belonged on my altar a reminder of the land's quiet wisdom. Bringing it home, I nestled it beside a feather I had found on my travels, a gift from the unseen. In moments like these, I sensed the whispers of the divine feminine, not in grand revelations but in the quiet assurance that I was held, guided, and deeply connected.

The objects we choose for our altars hold significance beyond their physical form; they become vessels of meaning, woven with intention and memory. A crystal gifted by a friend, incense from a sacred temple, or a small photograph of an ancestor each carries an essence of devotion, a reminder of the sacred within and around us.

In the sacred dance of daily life, there exists a space where the physical meets the spiritual a sanctuary where the divine whispers are heard amidst the mundane. This space, your altar, is a deeply personal place of communion with the soul's deepest knowing, a portal to the infinite realms of spirit. Uniquely yours, it serves as a reflection of your soul's journey and a focal point for your spiritual intentions.

ALTARS

Altars have been revered throughout history, as tools of connection and transformation. They honour ancestors, spiritual guides, the elements, and divine beings, creating a bridge between the seen and unseen worlds. When we create an altar with intention, we engage in a sacred act of communication a transmission of our desires, hopes, and prayers, and an invitation to receive guidance and blessings.

The objects you choose to place on your altar are less significant than the meaning you imbue them with. Whether it's a photograph, a piece of pottery, or a cherished keepsake, each item should symbolise your focus and resonate deeply with your spiritual journey.

Altars for a Purpose

Altars serve as powerful focal points for many purposes: initiating new beginnings, cultivating relationships, attracting abundance, encouraging fertility, promoting health, uniting communities, celebrating life's milestones, charging sacred tools, and directing or dispersing energy.

Your altar can take many forms, reflecting either a general approach to your spiritual practice or focusing on specific aspects of your journey. There are no rules or limitations, only the freedom to create a space that feels alive with meaning.

A general altar serves as a space dedicated to all your spiritual intentions, incorporating elements that resonate with your spiritual path. This might include candles, crystals, sacred texts, and symbols representing the divine in many forms.

A specific altar is dedicated to a particular intention. It may be dedicated to a specific deity or created as a focal point for an aspect of your spiritual growth. For example, you might create an altar for healing, love, wisdom, or protection.

A healing altar might be adorned with items that promote physical and emotional healing, healing crystals, herbs, and a bowl of water from a sacred spring or well. Each specific altar is imbued with symbols and items that align with that particular focus, supporting you through a particular phase of life or challenge. I create special altars from the New Moon to the Full Moon to gather energy and from the Full Moon to the New Moon to release it, allowing the cyclical flow of energy to guide my spiritual focus.

THE MANDALA OF WISDOM: A GUIDING STRUCTURE

In spiritual traditions, a mandala is a sacred geometric pattern representing the universe, a tool for focusing the mind and invoking deeper states of consciousness. The Mandala of Wisdom can serve as a powerful framework when designing your altar. It symbolises your inner world, guiding you toward clarity, insight, and enlightenment.

To create an altar using the Mandala of Wisdom as a guide, you could consider invoking the qualities of the four directions with an object from nature:

- **East:** Symbolises new beginnings, inspiration, and the dawn of awareness. An image of a sunrise, a yellow candle, or a flower in bloom are symbols to draw in the energies of fresh starts and creativity, or a feather to represent the element of air.
- **South:** Connected to passion, transformation, and the element of fire. You might place red candles, a small cauldron, or a representation of a phoenix, embodying the power of change and the fire of the spirit.
- **West:** Associated with emotions, intuition, and the element of water. A bowl of water, a moonstone, or a seashell can evoke the qualities of the west, cultivating healing, and emotional balance.
- **North:** Represents wisdom, clarity, and mental focus. On your altar, this direction might include symbols such as a clear quartz crystal, an open book, flowers, or a plant, connecting to the element of earth.

At the centre of the mandala on your altar you can place an object that represents your highest self or the divine connection you seek to honour. This could be a statue of a deity, a sacred symbol, a photo of you as a child, your inner child, or even a mirror, reflecting the divine light within.

PLACEMENT

When creating an altar, let your intuition guide you to a place in your home where the energy feels still, serene, and receptive. This could be a corner bathed in soft morning light, a secluded niche, or even a simple shelf. What matters is how it makes you feel, invited, anchored, present.

SELECTING SACRED OBJECTS

An altar is composed of elements that resonate with your spirit. Each item you choose should carry a meaning that is deeply personal to you.

- **Candles:** Symbolising the light of wisdom and the illumination of truth, candles bring warmth and a sense of the sacred to your altar. Take care to burn a candle on a heat proof dish or container and remember to blow out your candle after your prayer or invocation, never leave a flame unattended, or where pets or children can reach it.
- **Crystals:** Representing the earth's natural beauty and power, crystals hold specific energies that amplify your intentions and align your vibrations.
- **Incense or Herbs:** The smoke from incense or

smouldering herbs carries your prayers to the heavens, purifying the space and inviting in higher frequencies.
- **Sacred Texts or Symbols:** Whether a beloved book, a sacred scripture, or symbols that represent the divine to you, these elements connect your mind and heart with the wisdom of the ages.
- **Offerings:** Fresh flowers, a bowl of spring water, or a piece of fruit can be placed on your altar as offerings, symbolising your gratitude and humility before the divine.

As you arrange your altar, let your hands move with intuition and love. Balance is not perfection, it is feeling.

AWAKENING THE SACRED WITHIN

Creating and tending to your altar is a practice of mindfulness and devotion. Each time you light a candle, place an offering, or say a prayer, you activate your intention and awaken the sacred. Your altar becomes a mirror of your soul and s sanctuary for your becoming.

Reflection
- What would you like your altar to represent or amplify in your life?
- How can the process of creating and tending to an altar help you connect with your intentions and the divine?

Closing Affirmation
I create a sacred space where my intentions, prayers, and gratitude meet the divine. My altar is a sanctuary for my soul, a portal to infinite wisdom, and a reflection of the sacred light within.

CHAPTER 3
GATHERING: THE ART OF HOLDING CIRCLE

My first experience of sitting in a sacred circle was during a Red Tent training in 2005. At the time, I had never encountered anything quite like it. As I entered the space, I was welcomed with a sacred ritual that I will never forget. My feet were gently washed in rose water, an act of reverence that felt both grounding and humbling, honouring and up lifting. As the fragrant water flowed over my skin, I felt layers of tension dissolve, replaced by a deep sense of being held and honoured.

As the cleansing ritual continued, I was smudged with sacred herbs, their cleansing smoke wrapping around me like an ancient blessing. The scent of sage and sweetgrass filled the air, clearing away unseen burdens, energies I hadn't even realised I was carrying. I was being prepared to step into a space that transcended the ordinary a sacred container where time felt like it softened.

When I took my place in the circle, I felt an ancient power awaken within me, something primal and profound. There was a rhythm to the gathering, an unspoken understanding that connected us all. Each woman shared her truth, her story, and her heart, while the others listened with reverence and without judgment. The vulnerability, authenticity, and trust that was shared in that space were unlike anything I had ever experienced.

It felt as though I had tapped into an ancient lineage, a thread of wisdom and connection that stretched back through generations. In that moment, I realised the immense power of the circle not just as a gathering, but as a sacred portal for healing, witnessing, and collective transformation.

That first experience planted a seed within me. It inspired me to honour the tradition of the circle and carry it forward into my own life and work. Looking back now, I see how that initial moment of sitting in circle has influenced so much of what I do, from holding sacred space to creating a Mandala of Wisdom that continues to connect and empower women across the world.

THE SACRED LEGACY OF CIRCLE

Throughout history, women have gathered in sacred spaces to share, heal and draw on the inner wisdom residing within each of them. The circle, an ancient and potent practice, is a ritual that connects us across time, offering solace amidst the overwhelming demands of modern life. The circle is more than a social gathering, it is a community; a resource to ground us in the present, strengthen our connection to the divine, and nourish our souls.

Holding sacred space is a profound and transformative art, that is not always covered in yoga teacher training or courses for other spiritual disciplines. It has the power to deepen the spiritual experience for all involved, creating a safely held sacred space and sanctuary where collective wisdom can flourish.

Within the sacred space of a women's circle, the ritual begins long before the first word is spoken. The act of gathering with intention transforms an ordinary meeting into a sacred event. Each element of the circle, from the space you choose, to the objects you bring, to the words you speak, is imbued with meaning.

To hold a sacred circle is to step into a role that carries responsibility and is an honour. As a facilitator, your role is to hold this space with reverence, ensuring that every woman who enters feels the power and sanctity of the circle. It is about recognising the sanctity of the space and creating an environment where every woman feels seen, heard, recognised and cherished.

It is a place where the soul exhales.

This chapter will guide you through the profound process of holding a circle, equipping you with the tools, insights, and wisdom needed to cultivate this ancient practice in your life and the lives of others.

SETTING THE TONE FOR THE GATHERING

At the beginning of my annual retreat, we gather in a sacred circle to perform a ritual that sets the tone for the weekend ahead. It begins with a moment of stillness, grounding ourselves in the present, and opening our hearts to the sacred space we are creating together. Then each woman is given a piece of paper for her own story of letting go and calling in and invited to write down something she is ready to release it may be a fear, a limiting belief, or a burden that no longer serves her. This act of reflection and release is deeply personal yet powerfully amplified by the collective energy of the circle.

As the fire crackles in the centre of our gathering, we take turns approaching the fire, holding our paper as if cradling a weight, we are ready to let go of. Some people read their words aloud, their voices shaking with sacred courage. Others choose silence, letting the flames consume their burden in a quiet, private act of release. The sound of the paper burning, the sight of it curling into ash, feels like a physical manifestation of letting go a tangible reminder that transformation begins with release.

Once the last piece of paper has burned, we shift to the next step: calling in. On a fresh piece of paper, each woman writes what she wishes to invite into her life over the retreat and beyond. Whether it is courage, love, abundance, or clarity, the act of writing becomes a declaration, a commitment to herself. One by one, we read these intentions aloud, placing the papers on an altar at the centre of the circle.

This ritual initiates the retreat. It anchors the container in reverence, trust, and possibility.

It reminds us: *Transformation begins in presence. Magic begins when women gather with intention.*

Creating Sacred Space

With the intention set and the energy of release and calling in has been activated, the next step in holding a circle is the creation of sacred space. Whether you are gathering in a yoga studio, a private home, or beneath the open sky, the space you create becomes the foundation for the circle's energy. Preparing this space with care and intention sets the tone for the gathering and honours the sacred work to be done.

Sacred space is not just a location. It is a vibration. It is how the space makes people feel, held, softened, safe to show up fully.

CLEANSING THE SPACE

The process of creating sacred space often begins with cleansing. Physically sweep and clean the area to ensure it feels fresh and welcoming, then move on to energetic cleansing. Smudging with sacred herbs like sage, palo santo, or sweetgrass is a sacred practice among many cultures. The smoke symbolically clears the air of any stagnant energy transmuting it. As you cleanse, move intentionally through the space, speaking prayers or affirmations of protection and harmony.

This can be as simple as saying: *May this space be a sanctuary of peace and transformation. May all who enter feel held, honoured, and safe.*

If smoke isn't practical for the space, an aura spray infused with essential oils like lavender, frankincense, or rosemary can uplift the air and invite purity into the space. You are not just cleansing the room. You are preparing the temple.

ARRANGING THE CIRCLE

Once the space is cleansed, arrange the seating in a circle a timeless symbol of equality, unity, and shared energy. Every woman equal. Every voice welcome. At the centre, place a focal point to anchor the circle's energy. This could be a candle, a crystal, a bowl of water, flowers, an altar on the floor or on a table, or any sacred object that resonates with your intention for the gathering. The focal point serves as a visual reminder of the collective energy and the purpose of the circle. Let this centre hold the collective energy. Let it become a heartbeat for your gathering.

Personalising the Space

Infuse the space with personal touches. Fresh flowers, meaningful symbols that reflect the intention of the circle, or seasonal decorations can add beauty and resonance. Invite participants to contribute to the sacred space by bringing objects that hold personal significance to them a photograph, a token, or a small offering for the altar. When women co-create the altar, they enter not as guests, but as keepers of the space. Add seasonal flowers, textures, music, candles let the energy reflect the intention. Let beauty become a bridge into stillness.

Opening the Circle

Begin the gathering with a ritual that signifies the opening of the sacred space. This could include a process of chanting or breathwork.

- **Calling in the Directions:** Invite the energies of the four cardinal directions East, South, West, and North and the elements they represent Air, Fire, Water, and Earth, to preside over your circle gathering.
- **Grounding:** Guide the participants on a grounding meditation to help them settle into the space.
- **Breathwork:** Guide participants through a short breathing exercise to calm and slow down and to synchronise the group.
- **Chanting or Singing:** A group chant or song can unify the group's energy and focus.

As the circle opens, invite each participant to silently set their own intention for the gathering.

A Quiet Truth to Remember

You don't need a title to hold sacred space.
You need presence.
You need trust.
You need to remember that when women gather, the portal opens on its own.
You are not creating magic.
You are remembering how to hold it.

Chapter 4
Holding Safe Space in a Sacred Circle

In our morning yoga class, which we lovingly call our Yoga Spirals, women from all parts of the world have come together to hold sacred space. In the circles I facilitate, I often begin by asking participants why they have chosen to attend. The answers are as diverse as the women themselves.

Some come simply to breathe, to be enveloped in loving feminine energy. Some are navigating challenging times and seek the nurturing environment of the circle to process their emotions. Others crave a space where they can form real, soul-deep connections free of judgement, hierarchy, or performance.

What unites every participant is the desire to be seen. To be met. The circle offers that. It is a return to the self through the mirror of others. A space where the sacred doesn't live above, but among us.

In Circle, each woman embarks on a unique journey of self-discovery, where a heightened awareness of herself and the pattern in her life becomes inevitable. She begins to observe how she relates and responds in relationships; she reassesses decisions she has made and becomes keenly aware of recurring patterns that play out in her life.

The knowledge that she will share her experiences each week often sparks a sense of accountability. This can manifest as motivation to embrace positive change and deep healing, or it may bring hidden resistance to the surface, to be faced. Either way, this process acts as a powerful catalyst for transformation, allowing each woman to confront and navigate her inner landscape with newfound clarity and intention.

THE WISDOM OF THE CIRCLE: WHAT WOMEN SAY

When I asked the women of my Mandala of Wisdom a global circle who have shaped this work what makes a circle truly sacred, they named qualities that go beyond facilitation. They spoke of how the energy feels, how their nervous systems settle, how they come home to themselves. Here is what they shared as essential:

What Makes a Circle Sacred

- **Community and Belonging:** A circle is a place where every woman feels a profound sense of belonging, where community supports both individual and collective growth.
- **Creating Stillness and Presence:** The circle offers a space to slow down, be still, and be fully present, cultivating a connection with the self and the divine.
- **Unconditional Love:** The foundation of the circle is unconditional love, where each woman is accepted for who she is, and her journey is honoured.
- **Protection:** Creating and maintaining a protective energy around the circle ensures that it remains a confidential, safe and sacred space for all participants.
- **Mindfulness and Presence:** Being fully present in the moment enhances the sacredness of the circle, allowing participants to connect more deeply with themselves and the collective energy of the group.
- **Honouring Your Body and Feelings:** The circle supports your unique expression and encourages you to honour

where you are at any given moment.
- **Moving from Head to Heart:** Encouraging participants to transition from intellectualising their experiences to feeling and embodying them, deepens the impact of the practices.
- **Generosity and Self Care:** Balancing giving of oneself to the group while also honouring and meeting one's own needs, is vital to sustaining personal and collective well being.
- **Trust in the Process:** Trusting in the process without needing to control or predict outcomes allows for organic growth, healing, and revelation.
- **Non Judgemental Space:** The circle must be free from judgment, serving as a sanctuary where everyone can express themselves authentically and vulnerably.
- **Embracing Vulnerability:** The circle is a safe space to embrace vulnerability, cultivating deep connections and authentic relationships, allowing healing to occur at a profound level.
- **Creative Integration:** Finding ways to blend ancient teachings with sacred rituals enriches the circle, keeping it alive and relevant to each participant.
- **Reflection and Integration:** Reflection after each session helps participants integrate their experiences into daily life, translating the transformative energy of the circle into lasting change and personal growth.
- **Consistency:** Regular gatherings create a rhythm and reliability that cultivates deeper connections and builds trust.

GUIDING PRINCIPLES

With the sacred space established, the circle becomes a container for transformation and healing. The energy of the circle is shaped by the agreements and principles that guide all the participants.

These guiding principles are the foundation of any sacred circle, ensuring trust, safety, and mutual respect. They create an environment where every participant feels valued, supported, empowered and safe to share authentically.

The first gathering is an opportunity to dedicate time to discussing and establishing the guiding principles for your circle. These principles should reflect the values of the group and provide a framework for how participants interact and engage within the space. When women co create the ground rules, they co own the container.

ESSENTIAL GUIDING PRINCIPLES

Here are some foundational guiding principles to inspire your circle:

- **Integrity:** Transparency, honesty, and congruency are the cornerstones of all interactions within the circle.
- **Confidentiality:** What is spoken in the circle remains within the circle. This principle is essential for creating a safe space where participants feel free to share openly.
- **Trust:** Trust is the foundation upon which the circle is built. Each participant commits to honouring the space and the group's shared purpose.
- **Acceptance:** Diversity of experience and interpretation is welcomed and celebrated. Every participant's journey is honoured without judgment or comparison.
- **Loving and Nurturing Communication:** Speak and listen from the heart. Interactions are approached with the intention to uplift, nurture, and support one another.
- **Choice:** The circle respects each participant's autonomy.

No one is ever pressured to share or participate beyond their comfort level.
- **Authenticity:** Participants are encouraged to express their truth courageously and without fear of judgment.
- **Respect:** Boundaries are honoured, and interactions are grounded in mutual respect.
- **Empowerment:** The circle supports personal responsibility, encouraging each participant to take ownership of her actions and growth.
- **Joy and Celebration:** The circle is a space for joy, happiness, and celebration of life's sacred moments.
- **Adventure and Growth:** The circle is an ever evolving journey, embracing the adventure of personal and collective transformation.
- **Unconditional Love:** The foundation of the circle is unconditional love. Each participant is seen and valued for who she truly is, and her path is honoured without conditions.
- **Generosity and Self Care:** Balance the act of giving with self nurturing. Participants are encouraged to honour their own needs while supporting the collective.

Collaborating and Co-Creating the Principles

The most powerful guiding principles are those that resonate deeply with the group. Together, you create a space for personal growth and transformation. In your first gathering, it will help to set the intention and establish an atmosphere of co-creation, to allow time for a collaborative discussion. Invite participants to reflect on their values and what they need to feel safe and supported within the circle. This process ensures that the principles are meaningful to the group and invites a sense of shared ownership and commitment to the group's sacred space.

Guiding principles are more than a list they are the heartbeat of the circle, shaping its energy and interactions. As a facilitator, when you embody these principles in your actions and words, this generates trust and cohesiveness. As facilitator, your role is to model integrity, authenticity, and unconditional love, creating a ripple effect that inspires others to do the same.

Guiding principles are not static; they evolve alongside the circle. At the beginning of each gathering, take a moment to reaffirm the principles as a group. This could involve reading the statements aloud or inviting participants to share how the guiding principles supported them in the last circle and since the last meeting. Reaffirming the commitments and discussing their relevance to each of the participants, strengthens the group's connection and trust. With these principles as your foundation, the circle becomes a sacred container where every participant feels empowered to connect, grow, heal, and can integrate their experience.

THE POWER OF CONNECTION

Humans are inherently wired for connection; it is an intrinsic part of our genetic makeup to seek out and belong to a community. When we feel disconnected or isolated, our bodies trigger the fight, flight, or freeze response, and cortisol, the stress hormone, floods our system. When we experience genuine connection, our brains release oxytocin a hormone intimately tied to feelings of trust, safety, and overall well-being.

THE TRANSFORMATIVE POWER OF CIRCLE

The circle is a microcosm of the greater world, a reflection of the interconnectedness of all life. What happens in the circle is not separate from our daily lives; it is a mirror that reflects our inner truths, our challenges, and our growth.

By learning to hold space for others in the circle, we also cultivate the capacity to hold space for ourselves. To hold a sacred circle is to step into the role of a guide, a healer, and a keeper of wisdom. It is a journey that requires courage, compassion, and a deep commitment to the path of spiritual growth.

As you continue on this journey, the circle is always there for you as a place of refuge, a source of strength, and a wellspring of divine wisdom. Through the sacred practice of circle, you will have a space to transform your own life while contributing to the healing and awakening of the world.

THE SACRED CIRCLE COVENANT

The Covenant is a living document, a reminder of our shared commitment to creating a Circle of trust, empowerment, and unconditional support. As we come together in this sacred space, we remember these promises to hold each other with the utmost care and reverence.

I covenant to honour the sacred space of this Circle with integrity, compassion, and an open heart.

I will be kind, truthful and direct: I commit to speaking my truth with honesty and clarity, honouring my own voice and the voices of my sisters.

- I promise to take ownership of my actions: I recognise my personal responsibility within the Circle, and in my life, and I will hold myself accountable for my thoughts, words, and deeds.
- I will seek support when needed: I understand that asking

for help is a strength, and I will reach out to my sisters when I need guidance, comfort, or encouragement.
- I will respect your need for space: I acknowledge that there are times when solitude is necessary for personal reflection and healing, and I will honour your boundaries without taking it personally.
- My intention is to witness, not to fix: I will hold space for you to express your truth without attempting to change, fix, or judge your experiences or choices.
- I will listen with an open heart: Your words are valuable and will be met with my full attention and empathy, free from interruption or judgment.
- Confidentiality is sacred: What is shared within this Circle stays within this Circle. I will honour the privacy, and no words spoken here will be carried beyond these walls.
- I will speak no ill of you: I vow to refrain from gossip or negative speech about you to others, choosing instead to communicate directly and lovingly within the Circle if issues arise.
- I will celebrate your unique beauty and talents: I see and appreciate the divine light within you, and I will uplift and celebrate your gifts, recognising that we are each reflection of one another.
- I will stand in my authenticity: I will not diminish or alter myself to fit in. I will be true to who I am, and I will support and encourage you to do the same.
- I will nurture our collective growth: I am committed to the growth of our Circle, encouraging an environment where we can all thrive, heal, and evolve together.
- I covenant to embody love and respect: In all my interactions within this Circle, I will act with love, respect, and an understanding that we are co- creators of this sacred space.

SAFELY HELD SPACE

When creating your Mandala of Wisdom, you could consider the guiding principles and commitment to create a safely held space:

- **Location:** Choose a location that feels sacred to you and the group. Ensure it is a place where participants can feel comfortable and safe.
- **Intention Setting:** Begin each gathering with a clear intention. This intention will serve as the foundation for the circle's energy and focus.
- **Guiding Principles:** Establish the Guiding Principles that will govern your circle.
- **Ritual:** Incorporate rituals that resonate with the group to anchor the energy of the circle.
- **Inclusivity:** Ensure that your circle is a welcoming space for all women, regardless of their background or spiritual beliefs.
- **Commitment:** Encourage consistent attendance and engagement to build trust and deepen connections within the group.

Chapter 5

Opening Ritual: The Call to Sacred Living

Every spring, I hold a retreat at Florence House on the south coast of England — a sanctuary nestled among sloping gardens where primroses bloom and sea winds carry whispers of the sacred. The land feels like a threshold, a place where the everyday dissolves and the unseen draws near. It is here, in this liminal space, that we gather for our annual springtime retreat — a ritual of renewal, remembrance, and quiet rebirth. For many, it marks the true beginning of the year.

Long before anyone arrives, I begin weaving the field — holding the circle in my heart, listening for what it wants to become. The altar becomes our devotional centrepiece, adorned with stones, shells, my drum, and symbolic offerings for the spirit of the weekend. I move slowly, intentionally. Each cushion is placed with care, each flower arranged in quiet prayer. Goodie bags await each woman — handmade anointing oils, small treasures, chocolates, and whispered blessings tucked into each fold.

This retreat is where our global sisterhood — formed through years of online yoga circles and ancestral spirals — gathers in embodied presence. Women travel from all corners of the earth: Italy, Sweden, Ireland, the US, and across Britain. As they arrive, their voices hum through the house in a soft crescendo of anticipation, laughter, and sacred nerves. I welcome each one as she crosses the threshold — not just into the room, but into herself.

The circle begins to breathe.
Awareness gathers like mist before the dawn.
There is a pause. A potency. A hush that speaks of something ancient.
We all know: this is not just a retreat.
It is a rite of passage. A remembering. A return.

We have crossed a threshold.
When all are gathered, I close my eyes and attune to the unseen. With reverence, I raise the conch shell to my lips. Its sound rings out — three long, soul-deep calls:

One for the directions.
One for the realms.
One for the unseen ones who walk beside us.

It is a summons. A blessing. A bridge between worlds.

Then I speak the words of invocation, anchoring our collective intention into the bones of the space. Together, we chant the sacred tone — *Ahhh* — the sound of the open heart, the unified field. Our voices rise and merge into one vibration. In that moment, something shifts.

A resonance forms.
The atmosphere thickens with mystery.
The tone is set.
The octave begins.
This is the moment of remembrance.
Chills. Tingles. Activation.
The circle is open.
The journey begins.

WHY WE OPEN AND CLOSE WITH RITUAL

A ritual for opening and closing the circle can deepen the sense of sacredness and structure within the gathering. These rituals help set the tone at the beginning and bring closure to the energy at the end, framing the journey with presence and intention. As you embark on the journey through *The Mandala of Wisdom*, the first step is to set aside space for the connecting to the sacred. This opening ritual will help you create an environment of reverence, grounding, and intention. It will invite the divine energies to guide you through the teachings of the book, allowing you to align with your highest wisdom and step into your sacred living with clarity and grace.

You are not just reading; you are entering sacred space.

OPENING RITUAL
A Ceremony of Beginning

Create Sacred Space
Before you begin, take a moment to prepare your surroundings. Find a quiet, comfortable place where you can sit without being disturbed. Gather anything that will help you create a sense of sacred space. You may wish to light a candle safely under your watchful gaze, burn incense, or place any sacred objects that resonate with you. These could be crystals, a feather, a small bowl of water, or something you have gathered from nature whatever holds meaning for you.

As you prepare your space, consciously clear any distractions and create a space of peace and intention, allowing yourself to fully immerse in this ritual.

Grounding and Connection

Sit comfortably and close your eyes. Take several deep breaths, inhaling through your nose, holding the breath for a moment, and then exhaling slowly through your mouth. With each breath, feel your body relaxing and grounding into the earth. Imagine roots extending from the soles of your feet, reaching deep into the earth beneath you. With each breath, feel these roots growing stronger, anchoring you to the earth's energy. Allow this grounding to centre you in the present moment, connecting you to the wisdom and energy of the earth.

Invocation of Sacred Energy

Now invite the divine energies to enter your space. Speak aloud or silently say the following invocation, calling upon the sacred forces that align with your highest good:

"I call upon the Divine, the Sacred Feminine and Sacred Masculine, and the wisdom of the earth and the stars, to guide me on this sacred journey.

May this journey through The Mandala of Wisdom be one of deep healing, growth, and transformation.

I open myself to receive the teachings of the earth, the moon, and the universe, aligning with the highest truth and wisdom that resides within me.

May this book serve as a vessel of light, wisdom, and grace in my life."

As you speak these words, feel their energy filling your space, wrapping around you in a cocoon of light and protection. Trust that the energy of wisdom, love, and transformation is flowing freely toward you.

Setting Intentions

Take a moment to reflect on your intention for this sacred journey. What is it that you seek through your exploration of The Mandala of Wisdom? What are you hoping to learn, heal, or transform? It could be something specific, such as embracing the Sacred Feminine, cultivating more peace in your life, or deepening your spiritual practice. State your intention silently or say the words aloud. Here are some examples or you may choose one that resonates with your own intention:

- *"I intend to deepen my connection with sacred wisdom that flows through me."*
- *"I open myself to healing, growth, and balance in my body, mind, and spirit."*
- *"I commit to living with reverence, compassion, and integrity."*
- *"I commit to living in alignment with my highest purpose."*

Allow the intention to settle deeply into your heart, knowing that it is now set in motion. Feel it vibrate through your entire being, aligning you with the wisdom and transformative power of the journey ahead.

Sacred Seal

Now we complete this opening ritual by sealing the space and intention. With your hands placed over your heart, say the following words:

"With gratitude and reverence, I seal this sacred space, knowing that the wisdom I need will be revealed to me in divine timing. I

trust the journey ahead and open myself fully to the light of wisdom that shines within me and all around me."

As you say these words, feel your connection to the divine wisdom within you growing stronger. You are ready to begin.

Closing the Circle
To close this opening ritual, and safely seal the energies, gently blow out the candle (if you lit one), acknowledging that while the light has been extinguished physically, the light of wisdom continues within you to light the path. Sit quietly for a moment, feeling the energy of the ceremony settle within you. When you are ready, open your eyes and begin your sacred journey through *The Mandala of Wisdom*.

CLOSING CEREMONY FOR A SACRED CIRCLE
The Ceremony of Return

Just as the circle is opened with intention, we close with devotion. This is how we create the sacred vessel for transformation.

As we are approaching the end of the last day of our retreat, the space has shifted. The energy is softer now deeper, more luminous. Stories have been shared, tears have been released, laughter has echoed across the walls. Our hearts have opened as we shared together. There is a quiet strength.

As we gather for our final time, I trace the arc from where we began to where we now stand. I invite each woman to share, in her own way, how she feels now compared to how she arrived. Words like lighter, seen, rested, float into the space. Sometimes it's a word. Sometimes it's a look. Sometimes there are no words, it's just a hand over the heart.

We close the circle with grace, with deep gratitude, and with reverence for all that has unfolded. The spirits of the directions are released. The invisible threads that held us are gently released, knowing they have done their work. And then, the room shifts again.
The mats are cleared; the altar remains glowing in the corner. There is space to dance, to hug, to laugh. Farewells are said with full hearts, eyes brighter, spirits lifted. No one leaves quite the same.

The circle closes, but the work continues rippling through their lives like the petals of a rose opening long after the weekend has ended.

Reflection: Why We Begin This Way

This ritual marks the beginning of your spiritual journey with The Mandala of Wisdom. It creates sacred space, sets clear intentions, and invites divine wisdom to guide your path. As you continue through the chapters, you may return to this ritual whenever you feel the need to reconnect with your intention, centre yourself, and re align to your path in sacred living.

The journey that you are about to embark upon is one of transformation, growth, and alignment with your higher self. Honour the space you've created, and trust that with each step, you are living more fully in harmony with your soul's purpose.

Ritual Elements to Inspire Your Own Circles

Opening Rituals

- **Invocation of the Four Directions:** Begin by calling in the energies of the four cardinal directions East, South, West, and North along with the elements they represent: Air, Fire, Water, and Earth. This invocation grounds participants and aligns the Circle with the natural and cosmic forces.
- **Chanting or Singing:** A group chant or song can harmonise the energy of the participants, uniting their voices and intentions. Consider selecting chants that reflect the theme of the gathering or are easy for everyone to follow.
- **Breathwork:** Guide the group on a short breathing exercise to ground their energy and bring their awareness fully into the present moment. Even a simple breathing practice (inhale, hold, exhale) can help participants feel calm and centred.
- **Anointing or Smudging:** Offer participants the opportunity to be anointed with essential oils or smudged with sage or palo santo, symbolising purification in preparation to enter the sacred space. You might personalise this by allowing participants to choose the oil or herb that resonates most with them.

Closing Rituals

- **Gratitude Circle:** Invite each participant to share one thing they are grateful for from the gathering. This practice draws the Circle to a close and reinforces the positive energy cultivated within the Circle.
- **Closing Chant or Song:** End with a chant or song that mirrors the opening, creating a bookend effect that signifies the completion of the Circle. This repetition can provide a comforting rhythm and sense of ritualistic completion.
- **Grounding Meditation:** Guide the group through a

grounding meditation, encouraging them to reconnect with the earth and feel supported as they prepare to return to their daily lives. Visualising roots extending from their feet into the earth can be particularly effective to bring people back to their physical senses.
- **Release of the Directions:** If you began with an invocation of the Four Directions, it is important to close the Circle by thanking the elements and releasing these energies. This ensures the Circle is energetically sealed and that no residual energy lingers.

SYMBOLS AND TOKENS OF THE CIRCLE

Incorporating symbols or tokens within the Circle can add a tangible layer to the experience, providing participants with something physical to connect to the spiritual work they are doing.

- **Circle Token:** At the start of the Circle, pass around a small token (like a stone, shell, or crystal) that each participant can hold while they speak. This token becomes imbued with the collective energy of the group, serving as a tangible reminder of the gathering.
- **Blessing Bowl:** Introduce a blessing bowl into which participants can place written intentions, prayers, or blessings throughout the gathering. This bowl becomes a vessel of collective hopes and energies.
- **Personal Talismans:** Encourage participants to bring a small personal item to the Circle that holds significance for them. They can hold it during the Circle or place it on an altar to contribute to the shared energy. After the gathering, the item carries the Circle's energy back into their personal space.

GUIDED REFLECTION OR JOURNALING TIME

Incorporating a period of guided reflection or journaling can help participants deepen their personal insights and integrate the experiences of the Circle.

- **Guided Reflection:** After an intense sharing or activity, invite participants to reflect quietly on what they experienced or their intentions for the purpose of the Circle. Prompts such as "What resonated most deeply with me today?" can help guide their reflection.
- **Journaling:** Leave time at the end of the Circle for participants to journal about their experiences. Encourage them to write any thoughts and emotions and imagery that arose during the gathering.

THE POWER OF STORYTELLING

Storytelling is a potent way to connect with the wisdom of the past and the lessons of the present. Incorporating storytelling into your Circle can inspire participants and deepen their connection to the shared experience.

- **Sharing Personal Stories:** Encourage participants to share a personal story related to the theme of the Circle. This builds connection and vulnerability within the group.
- **Myth and Folklore:** Introduce a myth, legend, or folktale that resonates with the Circle's intention. These timeless tales often carry archetypal lessons that can spark meaningful dialogue.
- **Collective Storytelling:** Invite the group to co-create a story, with each participant adding a part. This playful

exercise co-creates creativity and encourages unity.

INTEGRATION OF NATURE

Connecting the Circle to the natural world can amplify the sacred energy and remind participants of their connection to the earth and all living beings.

- **Seasonal Celebrations:** Align your Circle gatherings with the cycles of nature solstices, equinoxes, or the phases of the moon. This deepens the group's connection to the rhythms of the Earth.
- **Nature Walks:** If possible, incorporate a walk in nature as part of your Circle. Even a brief walk can enhance mindfulness and connection to nature.
- **Elemental Focus:** Each gathering could focus on a different element Earth, Water, Fire, Air exploring its qualities and how they relate to the group's collective experiences. This provides a fresh perspective for each gathering.

AFFIRMATIONS AND DECLARATIONS

Closing the chapter with affirmations or declarations can empower the participants and reinforce the transformative power of the Circle.

- **Affirmation Cards:** Offer affirmation cards at the end of the gathering, featuring a positive statement or intention that participants can carry with them as reminders of the Circle's energy.

- **Group Declaration:** End the gathering with a group declaration or chant that embodies the collective intention of the Circle. This shared moment of unity leaves participants feeling connected and empowered.

Why It Matters

When we gather this way, with presence, with intention, with sacred rhythm. We don't just hold circle. We shift culture. We remember.

Each circle is a mandala. Each woman, a keeper of wisdom. Each gathering, a ripple in the sacred feminine rising.

This is your call to rise, to remember, and to lead.
This is your Mandala of Wisdom.

Chapter 6
Smudging: A Smoke Ritual for Creating Sacred Space

The first time I experienced the ritual of smudging, I was enveloped in the glow of the full moon, deep within the embrace of an ashram nestled in the foothills of the Himalayas. The memory is etched into my soul like a sacred tapestry, woven with the scents of the earth and the whispers of ancient wisdom.

As the moon bathed the ashram yoga room in its silvery glow, the air shimmered with an unspoken reverence, an energy both timeless and otherworldly. A woman draped in white robes approached me, holding a smouldering bundle of sage. The tendrils of smoke rose like ethereal threads, intertwining with the night sky.

She began the ritual, her movements slow and deliberate, and as the fragrant smoke curled around me, I felt its presence as something more than just scent or sensation, it was a language of the unseen, speaking in the hushed tones of healing and renewal.

The soft tendrils of smoke brushed against my skin, carrying the touch of unseen hands. I closed my eyes, and for a moment, it felt as though I had been transported back through time, standing among my ancestors in a sacred grove beneath the same celestial witness.

The experience was profound as though layers of heaviness I had unconsciously carried were dissolving, not just from my body but from the depths of my being.

The rhythmic chanting in the background wove a melody that resonated deep within me, amplifying the ceremony's potency. I could feel the smoke moving through me, unblocking pathways I hadn't even realised were closed. It was as though I had stepped into a lineage of seekers and healers, connected to a tradition far older than words. That evening, as I sat under the luminous moon, I understood the transformative power of ritual. Smudging was more than just a cleansing practice it was an invocation of the sacred, a bridge between the seen and unseen, an offering of devotion to something greater than myself. From that moment, smudging became an integral part of my spiritual practice, a ritual that continues to ground and uplift me to this day.

CREATING THE SACRED SPACE

Creating sacred space is a transformative journey that allows us to deepen our spiritual awareness of the energies within us and offers an opportunity to connect with the energies that unify our collective gatherings. The process of cleansing, clearing, and setting up the altar space is a ritual that transforms an ordinary space into a sanctuary for spiritual work.

CLEARING AND CLEANSING THE SACRED SPACE

Smudging or purifying the air around your home, temple, personal space, or body with smoke from smouldering aromatic herbs is a powerful ritual for cleansing energy, removing stagnation, and preparing a space for sacred work. This practice has been used for centuries across various spiritual traditions to clear negative energy and invite higher vibrations

How to Smudge a Sacred Space

- **Set Your Intention:** Before beginning, clearly state your intention for the cleansing. For example, you might say, "I release all stagnant or discordant energies from this space. May only love, harmony, and divine light reside here." Setting an intention directs the energy of the ritual and strengthens its impact.
- **Connect with Spirit:** Acknowledge the sacredness of the plants, crystals, or elements you are working with. Offer gratitude to the spirit of the herbs for their healing properties and protective energies.
- **Light the Smudge Stick:** Use a match or candle to ignite the smudge stick or loose herbs in a fireproof vessel, such as a clay pot or shell. Allow the flames to catch, then gently extinguish them, allowing the embers to smoulder and release their fragrant cleansing smoke.
- **Purify Your Energy:** Holding the smouldering bundle, gently waft the aromatic smoke around your body, beginning at the crown of your head and moving downward to your feet. Imagine the smoke dissolving any heaviness or negativity, leaving behind clarity, peace, and alignment.
- **Smudge the Room:** Using a feather or your hand, guide the smoke throughout your space. For a thorough cleansing, start at the entrance and move in a clockwise direction around the room, allowing the smoke to reach all corners, doorways, and windows. You may wish to chant or pray as you do this, inviting in protection and divine presence.

ENHANCING YOUR SACRED SPACE

Creating and maintaining a sacred space, aligned with the Mandala of Wisdom, serves as an energetic sanctuary, a place where intention, focus, and transformation can unfold. This space offers a refuge of serenity, a portal for deep contemplation, and a foundation for sacred work. It cultivates mindfulness, amplifies inner harmony, and strengthens your alignment with the divine currents that flow through all things.

In harmony with the principles outlined in The Mandala of Wisdom, your sacred space can be imbued with greater intentionality and spiritual depth by incorporating elements that align with ancient wisdom and the natural world. These elements serve as energetic anchors, creating balance and resonance within your altar space:

- **Fire:** Symbolised by the transformative power of a candle's flame, representing the radiance of the sun, or an image of fire calling upon illumination, passion, and purification.
- **Earth:** Grounded in the stability of crystals, stones, sacred soil, or a plant or flower to represent the nurturing growth of earth connecting you to the wisdom of the earth and the cycles of nature.
- **Water:** In a bowl of water, a seashell, inviting emotional clarity, intuition, flow, and the fluidity of life's experiences.
- **Air (East):** Symbolised by a feather, incense, or a bell—calling upon inspiration, the breath of life and the new beginnings.
- **Spirit (Centre):** Placed at the heart of the altar, a sacred statue, of a deity, a symbol, sacred mala beads, or a personal totem to create a connection to the divine.

THE RITUAL OF OPENING: SUN WISE

Honouring the natural cycles of the cosmos enhances the energy of your altar. Moving clockwise sun wise aligns you with the path of the sun's daily journey across the sky. Even during the waning phases of the moon, this direction embodies expansion, growth, and the illumination of consciousness.

Before engaging in spiritual work, take a moment to centre yourself. Close your eyes, inhale deeply, and exhale slowly, allowing yourself to arrive fully in the present moment. As you approach your altar, move sun wise turning to the right to activate the space. This mirrors the cycle of the rising sun, calling upon clarity, vitality, and divine manifestation.

These sacred gestures are ways to open your sacred space:

- Lighting a candle, inviting the presence of divine light.
- Burning incense, allowing fragrant smoke to carry prayers and intentions into the unseen realms.
- Placing your hands over your heart in reverence, anchoring yourself
- in love and presence.
- Set a clear intention for your time at the altar. Whether it is a prayer, a moment of gratitude, or a call for guidance, let your words resonate within you as a sacred invocation.

A BRIDGE TO THE DIVINE

Each time you sit at your altar, you engage in a sacred conversation with the universe, the ancestors, the divine, and your own inner truth. This isn't performance. *It's a remembering*. Returning to this sacred space for a moment of stillness, in your day, a breath of gratitude, or for daily meditation, creates a rhythm that nurtures your spiritual unfolding. These daily rituals are a bridge between your inner world and the divine. Spiritual path is not a distant destination, it's a journey through life, unfolding in each breath, each quiet moment of connection.

- **Morning intentions** – Begin your day by lighting a candle and setting an intention for how you wish to move through the day.
- **Evening reflections** – Close your day with gratitude, offering thanks for the lessons, moments of joy, and insights received.
- **Journaling and divination** – Pull an oracle card or write reflections in a sacred journal to receive guidance and deepen your awareness.

CLOSING THE ALTAR: MOON WISE

When your practice is complete, closing the space is just as sacred as opening it. To seal the energy and bring it back to stillness, move moon wise (counter-clockwise) to honour the waning moon's descent into introspection, rest and receptivity.

To close the altar session:

- Extinguish the candle, honouring the light within you that continues to shine.
- Offer words of gratitude for the insights and presence received.
- Place your hands together at your heart centre, bowing in reverence to the divine within and around you. This final gesture of gratitude and reverence acknowledges the cyclical nature of life where every act of creation is followed by a period of rest and renewal.

EMBRACING THE JOURNEY

The power of your altar lies in the consistency of your presence. It is not just a practice, it is a relationship.

Creating and tending to an altar is more than a spiritual practice, it is a living, breathing relationship with the sacred. It invites the divine into the fabric of your daily life, weaving the mystical into the ordinary, and grounding you in the eternal presence of the unseen.

As you continue this journey, let your altar be a sanctuary of remembrance, a place where your spirit finds refuge, where your heart speaks, and where your soul is nourished. In this space, in a corner of your home, you are reminded that every moment is sacred. Every breath is a prayer. And with each step you take, you walk the path of wisdom, grace, and divine love.

Chapter 7

Treasures for the Altar

One spring morning, just before a retreat, I took my usual walk along the beach. The pebbles shifted underfoot, and the waves, icy and sharp, pulled and released like the breath of the earth herself.

As I gazed down at the tide-washed stones, I saw it. A smooth, weathered Hag Stone, its hole perfectly carved by time and water. Something in me stilled. I bent down, lifted it from the sand, and traced my fingers over its contours. There was a presence to it, a silent whisper carried by the wind. I held it up to my eye and peered through the opening, and in that small, intimate moment, I felt as if I were glimpsing something beyond the veil of the ordinary. It felt as though it had chosen me, rather than the other way around. I slipped it into my pocket, and from that moment forward, it became a constant companion.

The Hag Stone: A Portal Between Worlds

One of my sacred tools found me, when I least expected it; the Hag Stone, discovered on the windswept shores of the beach, just before setting up the altars and opening the circle circle for this spring retreat. It has been with me through countless meditations, resting in my palm as I entered stillness. It has been beside me in coaching calls, a quiet anchor when words flowed between souls seeking deeper truths.

There is something about the weight of it, the coolness against my skin, that connects me to something vast and unseen. It reminds me that wisdom often arrives unbidden, carried by the tides of time, waiting for us to notice.

I think of that morning often, of how I could have walked past, unaware of the small gift waiting to be found. But I didn't miss that moment. I saw it. I held it. And in doing so, I was reminded that life is always offering us sacred tools, if only we have the eyes to see them.

The Hag Stone remains with me to this day. A small, unassuming piece of the earth that has become a threshold, a reminder, a talisman. And as I hold it, I wonder what sacred tools are waiting to find you?

THE WISDOM OF THE HAG: GUARDIAN OF THRESHOLDS

The presence of this stone in my life deepened my connection to the archetype of the Hag, an ancient figure of wisdom and transformation. In her book Hagitude, Sharon Blackie speaks of the Hag not as the fearful old woman of fairytales, but as the wise one, the guardian of cycles, the keeper of the liminal. She is the voice of the land itself, the breath of the wild, the one who has walked through fire and emerged carrying the embers of truth.

Hag Stones also known as Adder Stones, Witch Stones, or Faery Stones are regarded as objects of protection, vision, and ancient wisdom. Folklore speaks of their ability to offer second sight, to reveal the unseen, to act as a threshold between worlds. In some traditions, they were tied to doorways to guard against spirits; in others, they were carried as talismans by those who walked the path of the mystic.

In many ways, this stone embodied that same energy. It was a teacher of patience, of trust, of seeing beyond first impressions. It taught me that objects can carry presence, that they can arrive in our lives as symbols of something deeper. This stone, smoothed by centuries of motion, carried echoes of the earth's own memory. And like the Hag, it was an invitation to see beyond, to listen deeply, to honour what is ancient within us.

Sacred Tools and the Journey Forward

As we embark on our journey along the spiritual path, specific tools appear that will serve as our companions, grounding us, guiding us, and helping us to connect with the divine. These sacred tools are not merely objects; they are extensions of our intentions, symbols of our inner work, and conduits through which we channel the energies of the universe.

Some tools come to us in moments of deep intention, a crystal chosen for its healing properties, a bell that calls us to meditation. Others arrive unexpectedly, carrying messages from the unseen world.

Sacred tools arrive in our lives in ways both ordinary and extraordinary. Some are chosen with care, others appear like signs along the way. What matters most is how we listen to them, honour them, and allow them to guide us. The journey is not about the tools themselves, but the sacredness we awaken within ourselves when we use them.

Crystals: Earth's Treasures

Crystals are among the most ancient and powerful of sacred tools.

Formed deep within the Earth over millennia, they carry the Earth's energy and wisdom, each crystal vibrating with its unique frequency. Crystals can be used for healing, protection, meditation, and enhancing spiritual practices.

- **Clear Quartz:** Known as the 'master healer', clear quartz amplifies energy and intention. It can cleanse, protect, and enhance the energy of other crystals.
- **Amethyst:** This purple stone is deeply connected to the third eye and crown chakras, aiding in spiritual awakening, intuition, and inner peace.
- **Rose Quartz:** Associated with the heart chakra, rose quartz promotes love, compassion, and emotional healing. It is a powerful tool for cultivating self- love and forgiveness.
- **Black Tourmaline:** A protective stone that grounds energy and shields against negativity. It is particularly useful during meditation or when working through challenging emotions.

Crystal Healing Ritual

- **Choose Your Crystal:** Select a crystal that resonates with your current needs. For example, if you seek emotional healing, choose rose quartz.
- **Cleanse Your Crystal:** Cleanse your crystal by holding it under running water or placing it in sunlight for a few hours.
- **Set Your Intention:** Hold the crystal in your hands and close your eyes. Set a clear intention for what you wish to achieve through this ritual.
- **Meditate with the Crystal:** Place the crystal on the corresponding chakra or hold it in your hands. Visualise its energy flowing into you, aligning with your intention.
- **Express Gratitude:** After your meditation, thank the crys-

tal for its energy and place it on your altar.
•

Candles: Flames of Intention

Candles, as symbols of the divine light within and around us, are versatile tools in your spiritual practice. When you light a candle, you are calling forth the flame of your intention, inviting the energies of transformation, clarity, and illumination into your space. Each colour carries its vibration, inspiring you to use candles in creative ways in your spiritual practice.

- **White Candles:** Symbolising purity and protection, white candles are used to cleanse and create sacred space, invoking divine light.
- **Red Candles:** Associated with passion, energy, strength, and courage. Red candles can be used in rituals of empowerment, love, and vitality.
- **Green Candles:** Green represents growth, healing, vitality, and abundance. Lighting a green candle can aid in manifestation and prosperity work.
- **Blue Candles:** Blue is the colour of communication, truth, and peace. Blue candles are used in meditations and rituals to enhance peacefulness, spiritual communication and to calm the mind.

A Candle Meditation

- **Select a Candle:** Choose a candle that aligns with your current intention.
- **Create a Sacred Space:** Light the candle and place it in front of you. Sit comfortably and take a few deep breaths to centre yourself.
- **Focus on the Flame:** Gaze softly at the candle flame, allowing your mind to quiet and your focus to deepen.

Visualise the flame illuminating your intention, sending your desires into the universe.
- **Meditate in Silence:** Spend a few minutes in silent meditation, feeling the warmth and energy of the candle's flame.
- **Close the Ritual:** When you are ready, extinguish the candle with gratitude, knowing that your intention has been set into motion.

INCENSE AND HERBS: THE BREATH OF SPIRIT

Incense and herbs are sacred tools that connect us to the elements of air and fire, purifying our space and elevating our prayers. The smoke from burning incense or herbs is believed to carry our intentions to the heavens, creating a bridge between the physical and spiritual worlds.

- **Sage:** Known for its cleansing properties, sage is often used to purify spaces, objects, and the aura. Smudging with sage can clear stagnant energy and invite higher vibrations.
- **Palo Santo:** This holy wood from South America brings blessings and positive energy. A sweet, uplifting scent is ideal for setting a sacred tone before meditation or ritual.
- **Frankincense:** A resin with ancient roots in spiritual practices, is often burned to enhance meditation, prayer, and spiritual connection. A deep, resinous scent is grounding and elevating, connecting you to a rich spiritual tradition and helping to open the third eye and crown chakras.
- **Lavender:** Known for its calming and healing properties. Burning lavender can bring peace, relaxation, and a sense of divine protection.

CREATING AN INCENSE RITUAL

Choose Your Incense: Select an incense that resonates with your intention. For example, use lavender for peace and relaxation.

- **Light the Incense:** Light the incense and allow it to smoulder. As the smoke rises, visualise it carrying your prayers and intentions to the divine.
- **Purify Your Space:** Walk around your space, allowing the smoke to cleanse and purify the energy. You can also pass the smoke over your body to clear your aura.
- **Sit in Reflection:** After smudging, sit quietly in the cleansed space, feeling the peace and clarity that the ritual has brought.
- **Sacred Sounds:** Vibrations of the Divine Sound has been used for millennia as a tool for healing and spiritual connection. Sacred sounds, whether through chanting, singing bowls, or bells, resonate with the vibration of the universe, aligning us with the higher frequencies of the divine.
- **Chanting and Mantras:** The repetition of sacred words or sounds can elevate consciousness, clear the mind, and open the heart. Mantras are powerful tools for focusing the mind and invoking divine energy.
- **Singing Bowls:** These metal or crystal bowls create a resonant sound when struck or played with a mallet. The vibrations from singing bowls can cleanse the aura, align the chakras, and deepen meditation.
- **Tuning Forks:** Tuning forks emit a pure tone that can be used to balance the body's energy fields and chakras. They are especially useful for sound healing and deep meditation practices.
- **Bells and Chimes:** The clear, crisp sound of a bell or chime can instantly shift the energy in a space, calling forth the presence of the divine. Ringing a bell before and after meditation or ritual can help to create and close sacred space.

SOUND HEALING MEDITATION

Choose Your Sound Tool: Select a singing bowl, bell, or tuning fork that resonates with you.

Create a Sacred Space: Sit comfortably in your sacred space. Take a few deep breaths to centre yourself.

- Play the Sacred Sound: Gently strike the singing bowl or ring the bell. Allow the sound to resonate through your space and your being, feeling the vibrations as they cleanse and align your energy.
- Meditate with the Sound: As the sound fades, sit in silence and observe any shifts in your energy or consciousness.

THE PENDULUM: A TOOL FOR GUIDANCE

The pendulum is a simple yet powerful tool for divination and spiritual guidance. It consists of a weighted object, often a crystal or metal, suspended on a chain or cord. You can receive answers from your higher self by asking questions and observing the pendulum's movements.

- **Choosing a Pendulum:** Select a pendulum that feels right to you, whether it's made of crystal, metal, or wood. The key is to choose one that resonates with your energy.
- **Using the Pendulum:** Hold the pendulum steady and ask it simple yes or no questions. The pendulum will begin to swing in a particular direction clockwise, counterclockwise, or side to side giving you the answers you seek.
- **Cleansing the Pendulum:** Like other sacred tools, the pendulum should be cleansed regularly. You can cleanse it by holding it under running water, passing it through incense smoke, or placing it on a bed of salt or crystals.

Pendulum Guidance

- **Set Your Intention:** Before using the pendulum, set a clear intention for the guidance you seek.
- **Hold the Pendulum Steady:** Sit quietly and hold the pendulum by its chain, allowing it to hang freely. Ask your question and observe its movements.
- **Interpret the Movements:** Notice the direction in which the pendulum swings. Clockwise may indicate "yes" while counterclockwise means "no" and swinging from side-to-side means "maybe". Trust your intuition in interpreting the answers.
- **Express Gratitude:** After receiving guidance, thank the pendulum and the spiritual energies that have assisted you.

Sacred Tools and Your Spiritual Journey

Each sacred tool is a thread in the intricate tapestry of your spiritual practice, offering support, guidance, and illumination as you navigate your path. These tools act as reminders of your connection to the divine, providing tangible ways to channel energy, set intentions, and align with your higher purpose. In their simplicity lies profound power. In your hands, they become conduits of transformation, helping you to step more fully into your authentic self and embrace the sacred in all that you do. By integrating them into your daily rituals, you create a rich, dynamic practice that evolves as you do.

Honouring the Tools

Caring for your sacred tools is an integral part of their power. These objects are living symbols of your intentions and energy. Honour your tools by:

- **Cleansing Regularly:** Use sunlight, moonlight, or sound to energetically cleanse your tools and keep them attuned to your vibration.
- **Storing with Care:** Place your tools in a dedicated space, such as a box, pouch, or altar, where they remain undisturbed and energetically protected.
- **Using with Intention:** Treat each tool with respect and use it with clear purpose, ensuring its energy remains aligned with your spiritual journey.

Creating a Personal Ritual Toolkit

You may feel called to assemble a personal ritual toolkit. This toolkit becomes a portable sanctuary you can take with you, allowing you to create sacred space wherever you are. This collection can reflect your unique spiritual path and include items that resonate deeply with your practice. A simple toolkit might include:

- Crystals, such as clear quartz, amethyst, or rose quartz.
- A candle for meditative focus or intention-setting.
- Incense or herb bundle for purification.
- A sacred text or journal for reflection.
- A singing bowl, bell, or chime for clearing and grounding energy.

Ethical Sourcing and Cultural Awareness

Incorporating sacred tools into your practice requires sensitivity and mindfulness. Many of these items are drawn from traditions that have deep cultural roots. Honouring the origins of these tools

includes:
- **Understanding Their History:** Take time to learn about the cultural and spiritual significance of the tools you use.
- **Sourcing Responsibly:** Support ethical suppliers who respect the environment and the communities that create these tools.
- **Using with Gratitude:** Approach each tool with reverence and a sense of responsibility, recognising it as a gift from the Earth or a sacred tradition.

INTEGRATION AND CONNECTION

The power of sacred tools does not come from merely owning them or adopting meanings assigned by others. Whether it's a crystal, a drum, or a Tibetan bell, their true significance is revealed through how you weave them into your personal practice, imbuing them with intention and sacredness.

By using these tools regularly and with purpose, you deepen your connection to the divine, enhance self-awareness, and align your actions with your higher path. Each time you light a candle, hold a crystal, or sound a bell, you are engaging in a sacred act a tangible expression of your spiritual commitment. Though seemingly simple, these moments create ripples of transformation, extending far beyond the ritual itself.

As you continue your spiritual journey, remember that the tools you use are companions, not the destination. They are there to guide you, to deepen your practice, and to remind you of the sacredness that permeates every aspect of life. Treat them as allies, honour their origins, and allow them to amplify the light and wisdom within you.

Chapter 8
Embracing the Elements

It was the Winter Solstice, the longest night of the year, and I found myself driving through the darkness with a friend, heading towards Stonehenge. Four times a year, this sacred stone circle opens to the public for a few fleeting hours, offering the rare chance to stand where the ancients once stood, to witness the celestial dance between Earth and sky.

The stars were still bright when we arrived, though parking was chaotic. We mounted a grass verge, left the car, and took the bus toward the site. As we approached, the energy of the celebration buzzed all around me drumming, voices chanting, a quiet reverence woven through the winter air. My feet were bare, the frozen ground anchoring me as I moved closer to the towering stones.

With great reverence, I approached one of them, pausing just before stepping into its energy. I asked for permission to enter, breathing deeply as I felt the earth's vibrations move up my legs an electric current straight from Gaia. My legs trembled, my heart pounded, and then, from somewhere beyond words, a knowing rose within me: "Enter."

I placed my hands tentatively upon the stone. It was as if my palms had been plugged into an ancient circuit, energy humming through them. Slowly, I brought my forehead to rest against the cool surface, my third eye pressing into the weathered rock. Something profound happened in that moment my body, my mind, and the stone merged. Time dissolved. I was no longer just standing in the present but sensing lifetimes unfurling before me, as if I had stepped through a portal into another world. For a heartbeat or perhaps an eternity the world stood still, and I stood with the stone.

It was here, in this moment of deep connection, that I truly understood what the ancients knew that we are intimately woven into the fabric of the cosmos, moving through cycles of birth, growth, transformation, and renewal, just as the Earth does.

The journey of life is not linear but cyclical, an ever-turning wheel of energy that connects us to the five elements Earth, Water, Fire, Air, and Ether.

These elements are more than symbolic forces; they are living energies that shape our existence, guiding us through different stages of awareness, transformation, and wisdom. They govern the natural world and the rhythms of our bodies, minds, and spirits.

This chapter is an invitation to step into this wisdom, to attune yourself to the great cycles of nature and the energies that flow through you. As we explore each element, we will journey through the solstices and equinoxes, the body's energy channels, and the essence of each element as it weaves its influence into our lives. By understanding and working with these cycles, we align ourselves with the sacred dance of creation, deepening our connection to the Earth, the cosmos, and ourselves.

ELEMENTAL BUILDING BLOCKS

The elements Air, Fire, Water, Earth, and Ether are the building blocks of the universe and the foundation of the mandala. Each element corresponds to a direction, a season, a time of day, and a phase of our spiritual journey, offering specific energies that we can work with in our daily lives:

- **Air:** Air represents mental clarity, communication, and intellect, and is integral to the process of growth and renewal. Represents the mind, communication, and breath. Air element is associated with the morning, the season of spring, and new beginnings. Air invites us to think clearly, speak our truth, and be open to new possibilities. Practices such as deep breathing exercises, chanting, express the element of Air. Working with essential oils such as lavender or eucalyptus can help us connect with the Element of Air, to bring clarity and inspiration into our lives.
- **Fire:** Represents energy, transformation, and willpower. Fire element is associated with the season of summer, midday, and the phase of action. Fire challenges us to take risks, pursue our passions, and embrace change. Rituals that include lighting candles, stimulates the Fire element, while engaging in sun ceremony rituals is symbolic of Fire. Incorporating spices like cinnamon or ginger into our diet can help us harness our inner Fire, igniting our inner drive and courage.
- **Water:** Represents emotions, intuition and healing. Water element is associated with autumn or fall, sunset and evening, and the mood of introspection and intuition. Water teaches us to flow with our emotions, listen to our intuition, and cleanse and heal our spirits. Rituals involving water, such as taking a ritual bath, drinking herbal teas, honours the Water element. Healing or intuitively work with crystals

such as amethyst or moonstone, can help us connect with the element of Water, restoring calm and emotional balance.

- **Earth:** Represents stability, grounding, and wisdom. Earth element is associated with winter, midnight, and the phase of completion. The Earth element encourages us to stay grounded, to honour our bodies, and reminds us to seek wisdom from the natural world. Practices like gardening, using grounding stones like hematite or onyx, or burning herbs like sage or cedar can help us connect with the grounding element of Earth, providing stability and support in our spiritual journey.
- **Ether (Centre/Spirit):** The element of Ether is the subtle essence that connects and unifies all other elements Air, Fire, Water, and Earth. Ether represents the space within which all creation exists. Ether is the medium through which spiritual transformation occurs. Ether represents the essence that connects and unifies all the other elements. Ether is the space within which all creation exists. It is also the medium through which spiritual transformation occurs. As the element of the centre, Ether embodies the unity of the mandala, integrating the energies of Air, Fire, Water, and Earth. Practices that enhance our connection to Spirit, such as meditation, prayer, or working with sacred symbols, help us to access the wisdom of Ether and bring harmony to our spiritual journey while allowing transformation to occur.

By working with these elements, we can create a balanced and harmonious spiritual life, attuned to the natural cycles of the Earth and our own inner nature.

Air represents mental clarity, communication, and intellect, and is integral to the process of growth and renewal. The elements are not separate from us they always move through us and around us.

- Earth stabilises us.
- Water softens us.
- Fire drives us.
- Air expands us.
- Ether connects us.

Every moment, we are invited to ask:

- What element am I embodying most right now?
- Which element do I need to call in for balance?
- Which element do I need more of today?

THE FIVE CYCLES OF AWARENESS
The Earth Cycle: Rooting in Stability

Earth is the stillness before movement, the pause before action. It holds us steady, reminding us that deep roots do not fear the wind.

When life feels uncertain, Earth asks: What is unshakable within you?

Sitting beneath an old oak tree, I once felt the weight of time pressing through its roots a patience that reminded me that strength comes not from force, but from endurance.

- **Practice:** Walk barefoot on the earth.
- **Journal:** What grounds me when life is uncertain?

THE WATER CYCLE: FLOWING WITH EMOTION

Water carries both stillness and movement. It is the river that carves through stone, not by force, but by surrender. There have been moments where emotions rose like tides, overwhelming in their force grief, love, longing. Water teaches that we are not meant to hold on too tightly that every feeling must have its flow. Sitting by the sea, watching the tide pull away, I once realised: what needs to leave will leave; what is meant to return will return.

- **Practice:** Bathe or sit near water.
- **Journal:** How do I allow my emotions to move freely?

THE FIRE CYCLE: IGNITING PASSION & TRANSFORMATION

Fire is raw power the moment an idea ignites into action. It is the spark of purpose, the courage to begin before everything feels certain.

We have all stood at that threshold knowing something must change but hesitating at the edge. I've felt that too, resisting the moment before stepping forward. But Fire does not wait. Fire insists: Act now. Begin now. And when I finally did? The energy shifted instantly, like striking a match.

- **Practice:** Light a candle with intention.
- **Journal:** What passion is waiting to be set alight?

THE AIR CYCLE: EXPANDING CONSCIOUSNESS

Air is the mind's vast horizon the element of breath, thought, and inspiration. It is the whispered idea before it forms into words, the first inhale before the voice speaks.
Have you ever had a moment where clarity strikes like lightning where suddenly, everything clicks? That's Air.

For me, it often comes in nature standing beneath an open sky, feeling my thoughts scatter like dandelion seeds, then rearrange themselves in perfect order.

- **Practice:** Breathe deeply. Let thoughts rise and settle.
- **Journal:** What ideas are ready to take flight?

THE ETHER CYCLE: MERGING WITH THE DIVINE

Ether is presence. It is the pause between the in-breath and the out-breath. It is the space between words, where silence holds the greatest truth.

There is no single moment where Ether is found it is found in every moment. I have felt it sitting in meditation, beneath a starlit sky in India, where the silence was so profound, it felt like the entire cosmos was listening. It is there in the stillness before sleep, in the quiet moments between thoughts.

- **Practice:** Sit in silence. Let the space itself become the message.
- **Journal:** How do I experience connection beyond the physical?

LIVING IN ELEMENTAL RHYTHM

When we live in tune with the elements, we remember, we belong to something ancient and wise.
- *Inhale and feel the Air.*
- *Exhale and ground into Earth.*
- *Light a candle, and welcome Fire.*
- *Sip tea and commune with Water.*

- *Sit in stillness and merge with Ether.*

You are not separate from nature. You are nature. The elements do not visit you. They live within you. And when you walk in elemental rhythm, every breath becomes a prayer. Every step a ritual. This is the way of the mystic. The way home.

Chapter 9
The Mandala as a Portal

In shamanic practices, the circle was seen as a portal between worlds, representing the cyclical nature of life, death, and rebirth. The Mandala is a map that helps the shaman navigate the spiritual realms and in-between states and bring back wisdom to the physical world. It is a tool for journeying, visioning, healing, and understanding the mysteries of existence.

It was during a retreat at sunrise that this truth first revealed itself in its fullness. The morning air was crisp, holding the last whispers of the night. We gathered upon sacred land, the damp earth cool beneath our feet, the sky painted with the first golden strokes of dawn. As we stood in stillness, awaiting the first movement, a knowing settled into my bones: we were standing at the centre of the mandala, a living embodiment of the ancient rhythm of existence.

Together, we began to move, honouring the sun wise and moon wise dance the eternal flow of masculine and feminine, action and surrender, outward and inward. Moving sun wise, we invoked the fire of the sun, the strength of the sacred masculine, the creative force of expansion that radiates outward. Moving moon wise, we surrendered to the quiet wisdom of the moon, the intuitive pull of the divine feminine, the spiral inward.

As we danced between these forces, something shifted. A stillness fell over the group. The wind picked up, swirling around us, as though carrying the energy of our practice out into the world. One of the women later shared a vision a spiral of light unfurling from the centre of our circle, weaving through each of us, linking us to something ancient, something infinite. In that moment, I understood: The Mandala is not just a practice. It is a portal.

A portal into unity, into remembrance, into the truth that every moment is an invitation to live in ceremony.

Creating a Mandala

A Mandala represents the sacred space you create with your circle to provide a place of balance, harmony, and divine connection. Each circle is an intricate design of energies, intentions, and shared experiences, which form a unique Mandala. As these circles are created around the world, they form a network of light, weaving together a global community of women committed to living sacred, intentional lives.

Ancient Roots: Shamanic Beginnings

The origins of the Mandala can be traced back to the earliest shamanic traditions, where symbolic circular designs were used in rituals and spiritual practices. Shamans, who were regarded by their village or tribe as the bridge between the physical and spiritual worlds, used these circles or sacred spaces to connect with the divine, to access other realms, and to bring healing and wisdom to their communities The Mandala is depicted as a circle within a square, symbolising the integration of the divine (the circle) within the material world (the square). This design reflects the balance between spiritual and earthly existence, a concept central to yogic teachings and shamanic traditions alike. For shamanic practices the Mandala serves as a representation of the sacred circle, the interconnectedness of life, and the gateway to the spiritual realm. It was a space where the shaman could journey into the spirit world, to communicate with ancestors, and gain insights into the mysteries of existence. The designs within these early Mandalas represent cosmic order, often reflected the shaman's deep connection with nature, depicting animals, plants, and celestial bodies in a way that expressed the interconnectedness of all life. This connection to nature is a core aspect of shamanic wisdom, symbolising harmony with the natural world and the cosmos.

THE MANDALA OF WISDOM AS A MAP OF SPIRITUAL EXPLORATION

The Mandala of Wisdom is more than an artistic design or symbolic pattern it is a living map of spiritual exploration, guiding us through the many layers of our existence. What begins as a simple practice a half sun salutation performed within a sacred circle gradually reveals itself as a profound ritual. Each movement unlocks a key, each breath activates a code, and each intention aligns with an internal frequency, drawing us deeper into the mysteries of the Mandala.

The Mandala of Wisdom encompasses layers of meaning; its shape and orientation to the Directions mirroring the meaning of the Inner Compass, the Elements, Moon Cycles, Phases of Womanhood, Times of Day, the Seasons, the Wheel of the Year, and the Divine Feminine. Each of these layers contributes to our journey towards greater self awareness and spiritual transformation. As we explore these layers, we begin to see their interconnectedness, weaving a rich tapestry of wisdom that we can draw upon in our daily lives.

Transformation at the Centre of the Mandala

In traditional mandalas, this central point is often symbolised by the bindu dot, which holds the infinite potential and wisdom of the entire universe. Within the Mandala of Wisdom, the practitioner is the living bindu, the focal point where all energies converge and from which all spiritual insights emanate.

At the heart of the Mandala of Wisdom the centre is a point of profound significance and power. This centre point is represented by the practitioner, who embodies the element of Ether or Spirit. Ether is the medium through which spiritual transformation occurs.

As the centre of the Mandala, the practitioner holds the wisdom of all the directions and elements, holding the space for transformation to take place, and integrating and harmonising these diverse energies.

This central position is not just symbolic, it is also practical, reflecting the practitioner's role in actively engaging with and balancing the energies of the Mandala. From their position at the centre, the practitioner navigates the layers of the Mandala with clarity and purpose, unlocking its deepest mysteries and integrating its wisdom into daily life.

By recognising them self as the centre of the Mandala, the practitioner aligns with the element of Ether, embracing their role as the keeper of the mandala's wisdom. This central point serves as the anchor, ensuring that all practices and insights gained from the Mandala are grounded in the unity and wholeness that Ether represents.

DIRECTIONS OF THE INNER COMPASS

The Directions of the Inner Compass are essential to navigating the Mandala of Wisdom. Each direction North, South, East, and West holds its own unique energy, guiding us through different aspects of our journey, while the practitioner, situated at the very centre of this compass, embodies the element of Ether or Spirit. The practitioner, like the bindu in traditional mandalas, is the central point where all energies converge and from which all spiritual insights flow.

- **East (Air):** The direction of beginnings, inspiration, dawn and the dawning of new ideas. This is where we awaken, set our intentions, and connect with the breath of life. Morning rituals such as journaling, meditation, and goal-setting are particularly potent when aligned with the East, as this direction helps ignite creativity and clarity.
- **South (Fire):** The direction of passion, action, and the energy of noon. Here, we are called to take bold steps towards our goals, ignite our inner fire, and embrace transformation. Practices such as dynamic yoga, dance, or any form of physical exercise are enhanced when oriented towards the South, as this direction fuels our motivation and courage.
- **West (Water):** The direction of introspection, emotions, and the setting sun. It is the place of healing, where we dive deep into our inner waters, release what no longer serves us, and connect with our intuition. Evening rituals such as reflective journaling, cleansing baths, or meditation are especially powerful when aligned with the West, as they help us process emotions and let go of the day.
- **North (Earth):** The direction of stability, wisdom, and the midnight hour. This is where we ground ourselves, connect

with our ancestors, and find the strength to stand firm in our truth. Grounding practices such as walking in nature, sitting in stillness, or working with crystals, resonate deeply when aligned with the North, as this direction provides the stability and wisdom needed for profound spiritual work.

- **Centre (Ether/Spirit):** The direction of the practitioner, representing the element of Ether or Spirit. The centre is the focal point of the Mandala, embodying the unity of all directions and elements. As the element of Ether, the practitioner integrates and harmonises the energies of Air, Fire, Water, and Earth, holding the wisdom of the Mandala within. This central point is where all spiritual insights converge, and where the practitioner anchors the insights and energies for the entire mandala.

By consciously aligning our practices with these directions and recognising the practitioner as the central point the bindu, embodying the element of Ether or Spirit we activate the Mandala's full potential. This ensures that our journey through the Mandala is balanced, harmonious, and deeply connected to the wisdom held within the Mandala's sacred structure.

THE ELEMENTS

The elements Air, Fire, Water, Earth, and Ether are the building blocks of the universe and the foundation of the mandala. Each element corresponds to a direction, a season, a time of day, and a phase of our spiritual journey, offering specific energies that we can work with in our daily lives:

- **Air (East):** Represents the mind, communication, and breath. Air element is associated with the morning, the season of spring, and new beginnings. Air invites us to think clearly, speak our truth, and be open to new possibilities. Practices such as deep breathing exercises, chanting, express the element of Air. Working with essential oils such as lavender or eucalyptus can help us connect with the Element of Air, to bring clarity and inspiration into our lives.

- **Fire (South):** Represents energy, transformation, and willpower. Fire element is associated with the season of summer, midday, and the phase of action. Fire challenges us to take risks, pursue our passions, and embrace change. Rituals that include lighting candles, stimulates the element, while engaging in sun-ceremony rituals is symbolic of Fire. Incorporating spices like cinnamon or ginger into our diet can help us harness our inner Fire, igniting our inner drive and courage.
- **Water (West):** Represents emotions, intuition and healing. Water element is associated with autumn or fall, sunset and evening, and the mood of introspection and intuition. Water teaches us to flow with our emotions, listen to our intuition, and cleanse and heal our spirits. Rituals involving water, such as taking a ritual bath, drinking herbal teas, honours the Water element. Healing or intuitively work with crystals such as amethyst or moonstone, can help us connect with the element of Water, restoring calm and emotional balance.
- **Earth (North):** Represents stability, grounding, and wisdom. Earth element is associated with winter, midnight, and the phase of completion. The Earth element encourages us to stay grounded, to honour our bodies, and reminds us to seek wisdom from the natural world. Practices like gardening, using grounding stones like hematite or onyx, or burning herbs like sage or cedar can help us connect with the grounding element of Earth, providing stability and

support in our spiritual journey.
- **Ether (Centre/Spirit):** Represents the essence that connects and unifies all the other elements. Ether is the space within which all creation exists. It is also the medium through which spiritual transformation occurs. As the element of the centre, Ether embodies the unity of the mandala, integrating the energies of Air, Fire, Water, and Earth. Practices that enhance our connection to Spirit, such as meditation, prayer, or working with sacred symbols, help us to access the wisdom of Ether and bring harmony to our spiritual journey while allowing transformation to occur.

By working with these elements, we can create a balanced and harmonious spiritual life, attuned to the natural cycles of the Earth and our own inner nature.

Moon Cycles

The Moon mirrors the cyclical nature of the Mandala and our spiritual journey. With its continuously changing phases, each phase of the Moon represents a different aspect of our path, offering unique opportunities for growth and reflection:

- **New Moon:** A time of new beginnings, setting intentions, and planting seeds for the future. The New Moon is an ideal time to start new projects, make plans, and focus on personal growth. Practices like writing down goals and setting intentions, performing manifestation rituals, or meditating on new possibilities can help to harness the energy of the New Moon.
- **Waxing Moon:** A time of growth, building energy, and moving forward with our goals. As the Moon waxes, our intentions gain momentum. This is the time to act, to pursue our goals with determination, and build on the

foundations we set during the New Moon. Working with affirmations, visualisations, or engaging in physical and practical activities that align with our goals, can help amplify the energy of the Waxing Moon.
- **Full Moon:** The time of peak energy, illumination, and the manifestation of our intentions. The Full Moon is a powerful time for celebrating achievements, gaining clarity, and seeing the results of our efforts. Practices such as Full Moon meditations, gratitude rituals, or moon bathing, spending time in nature under the moonlight, can help us connect with the Full Moon's energy, illuminating our progress and bringing insight and fulfilment.
- **Waning Moon:** A time of release, letting go, and reflection. As the Moon wanes, we are called to release what no longer serves us. This is the time to reflect on our journey and prepare for the next cycle. This is a powerful time for releasing and letting go, cleansing rituals, and for decluttering our space, or detoxifying the body. Engaging in introspection and reflection such as journaling and forgiveness practices, can help us align with the energy of the Waning Moon phase.

Aligning our practices with the moon cycles allows us to tap into the natural rhythms of the universe, enhancing our spiritual growth and personal transformation.

TIMES OF THE DAY

Each time of day corresponds to a different energy within the mandala, offering opportunities for specific spiritual practices:

- **Morning (East/Air):** A time of awakening, inspiration, and setting intentions. The morning is a powerful time to

connect with the energy of new beginnings, set the day's tone, and align with our highest intentions. Practices such as morning meditation, sun salutations, or writing in a gratitude journal can help us harness the morning's energy, bringing clarity and focus to our day.
- **Noon (South/Fire):** A time of action, energy, and making progress. The energy of noon is dynamic and powerful, making it an ideal time for acting on our goals, engaging in physical activities, and making decisions. Practices like a midday walk, energising yoga, or eating a nourishing meal can help fuel our bodies and minds, ensuring that we stay aligned with our purpose.
- **Evening (West/Water):** A time of reflection, relaxation, and healing. As the day winds down, the evening offers a space for introspection, emotional processing, and winding down. Practices such as reflective journaling, meditation, or a calming bath can help us to release the day's stresses and connect with our inner self, preparing for a restful night.
- **Midnight (North/Earth):** A time of deep introspection, grounding, and connection to the wisdom of the unconscious. Midnight is a sacred time for spiritual exploration, dreamwork, and connecting with the deeper layers of our psyche. Practices like meditation, working with crystals, or keeping a dream journal can help us access the unconscious mind's wisdom, offering insights and guidance for our spiritual journey.

Honouring the times of the day within our practice, we align ourselves with the natural rhythms of life, ensuring that we move through the mandala in harmony with the energies around us. Each time of day offers a unique opportunity to connect with specific aspects of our being, allowing us to create a balanced and holistic spiritual practice.

Seasons and the Wheel of the Year

The Wheel of the Year is a sacred calendar that marks the turning of the seasons and the cycles of nature. Each season is a gateway into a different aspect of the mandala, offering us opportunities to connect with the Earth's rhythms and to align our practices with the natural world:

- **Spring (East/Air):** Represents new beginnings, growth, and the renewal of life. Spring is a time of awakening, where the energy of the Earth begins to rise, bringing new life and fresh opportunities. It is celebrated during festivals like Ostara and Beltane, which honour the return of light and the fertility of the land. During this season, practices such as planting seeds, setting new intentions, or engaging in rituals celebrating growth and renewal are particularly powerful.
- **Summer (South/Fire):** Represents the peak of energy, abundance, and the height of the sun. Summer is a time of full bloom, where the Earth's energy is at its most potent, and everything is alive with vibrancy and activity. It is celebrated during Litha and Lammas, festivals that honour the fullness of life and the first harvests. During this season, practices such as celebrating the sun, engaging in creative projects, or harvesting the fruits of our labour help us connect with the energy of abundance and joy.
- **Autumn (West/Water):** Represents harvest, reflection, and preparation for winter. Autumn is a time of gathering, where we harvest what we have sown and prepare for the coming darkness. It is celebrated during Mabon and Samhain, festivals that honour the cycles of life and death and the turning inward. During this season, practices such as reflecting on the year's accomplishments, engaging in rituals of release, or honouring ancestors help us connect

with autumn's deep, introspective energy.
- **Winter (North/Earth):** Represents rest, introspection, and the rebirth of the sun. Winter is a time of stillness, where the Earth rests and prepares for the renewal of spring. It is celebrated during Yule and Imbolc, festivals that honour the return of the light and the deep wisdom found in the darkness. During this season, practices such as resting, meditating, or engaging in rituals that honour the cycles of life and death help us connect with winter's quiet, reflective energy.

The Wheel of the Year overlays perfectly with the Mandala, reminding us that our spiritual journey is intertwined with the cycles of the Earth and the cosmos. By aligning our practices with the seasons, we can create a spiritual practice that is deeply connected to the natural world, bringing us into harmony with the rhythms of life.

THE EVOLUTION INTO A SACRED PRACTICE

While the traditional mandala remains a powerful spiritual symbol, its principles have gradually been adapted into a more dynamic, embodied sacred practice. The Mandala of Wisdom represents this evolution, taking the symbolic elements of the mandala and translating them into a framework for sacred living in daily life.

This practice embodies the mandala's essence a journey inward towards wholeness and into our connection with the divine while taking its symbolism with us into daily life. Through rituals, movement, breathwork, meditation and contemplation, the Mandala of Wisdom transforms the abstract, symbolic mandala into a tangible, experiential practice.

RITUALS: THE OUTER CIRCLES OF DAILY PRACTICE

In this evolved form, rituals correspond to the outermost circles of a traditional mandala. They are the foundational practices that ground us in the physical world while opening us to higher realms. Just as the outer rings of a mandala protect and contain the inner layers, rituals provide structure and sacredness to our daily lives, reminding us of our connection to the divine.

BREATHWORK: THE LIFE FORCE WITHIN THE MANDALA

In a traditional mandala, the central point represents the source of all creation the divine essence that permeates the universe. Breath is the life force that flows through us, just as the lines and patterns flow through the mandala, linking every part of our being to the whole.

Breathwork is the practice that connects us directly to this source. By conscious breathwork, we align ourselves with this divine essence, using the breath to cleanse, energise, and centre ourselves, just as the central point of a mandala anchors and unifies the entire design.

MOVEMENT: EMBODYING THE SACRED PATTERNS

Movement in the Mandala of Wisdom represents the flow of energy through the mandala's geometric patterns. Just as the shapes within a mandala guide the eye towards the centre, movement guides the body and spirit towards balance and alignment. This acknowledges that the body is not separate from the spirit but is a vessel for experiencing and expressing the sacred.

Movement, as yoga, dance or other mindful exercises, becomes a physical manifestation of the mandala's symmetry and flow, allowing us to embody the principles of harmony, and unity in a sacred context.

MEDITATION: THE JOURNEY TO THE CENTRE

Meditation remains at the heart of the Mandala of Wisdom, just as the centre is the focal point of a traditional mandala. This practice leads us inward, guiding us through the layers of our consciousness to the still, silent core where wisdom and peace reside.

It is in meditation that the symbolic and the sacred mandala converge, where the journey of the spirit is mirrored by the journey of the mind. This mindful practice becomes a method of inner stillness and a way to integrate the insights gained from rituals, movement, and breathwork. This still point is the moment when all elements come together, bringing us into deep communion with our inner self and the universe.

In its evolved form, the Mandala of Wisdom is a powerful tool for practicing meditation and reaching towards self-realisation.

Practitioners use the Mandala to focus the mind to transcend ordinary thought patterns and connect with higher states of consciousness. It acts as a visual mantra, guiding the practitioner towards deeper understanding and insight.

CONTEMPLATION: REFLECTING ON THE PATTERNS

Contemplation in the Mandala of Wisdom is the final stages of engaging with a traditional Mandala, when we step back to reflect on the design as a whole. This reflective practice allows us to integrate the wisdom gained from our rituals, movement, breathwork and meditation into our daily lives. Through the practice of contemplation, we can make sense of our journey, drawing connections between the different aspects of our practice and recognising the divine patterns that weave through our existence.

UNLOCKING THE SACRED CODES

What begins as a simple half-sun salutation in a circle evolves into a transformative journey through the layers of the Mandala of Wisdom. With each turn of the Mandala, we activate keys, codes, and internal frequencies that align us with the deeper truths of the universe and ourselves.

These layers, the Directions, Elements, Moon Cycles, Phases of Womanhood, Times of Day, Seasons, the Wheel of the Year, the Zodiac, and Archetypes, are interconnected, forming a beautiful web of spiritual practice.

By creating your own Mandala of Wisdom you can bring together a sacred circle that honours the divine feminine, cultivates deep connection, and supports spiritual growth in your community. Sharing these practices is an invitation to join this global web of transformation and empowerment, creating Mandalas of Wisdom that resonate across cultures and generations.

As you step onto the path of the Mandala of Wisdom, you will find that the more you engage, the more the mandala reveals. It is an ever unfolding journey, inviting you to sink deeper into your practice, discover hidden connections, and embrace the divine energies within.

The mandala becomes a mirror, reflecting your inner world and a key, unlocking the sacred codes of wisdom and transformation.

PART II
WALKING THE WHEEL

Chapter 10
Mandala Directions: Your Inner Compass

The deeper I immersed myself in my Celtic roots, the more I felt the undeniable pull to travel across the British Isles, seeking out the ancient places that whispered of forgotten wisdom. I longed to stand where my ancestors once stood, to feel the pulse of the land beneath my feet, and to align myself with the great ley lines, the sacred wells, and the stone circles that have held ceremony for centuries.

It was during one journey to the west that I found myself in Tintagel, a land of myth and mist, where the stories of Arthurian legend and the echoes of the old ways linger like a veil between worlds.

The cliffs of Tintagel rise dramatically against the sea, the wind howling through the ruins of a castle that still hums with magic. But it was not the castle that called me it was the wild, untamed land beyond it, a world untouched by time. I made my way toward St. Nectan's Glen, a place that had been whispered to me in dreams, a place where the veil between the seen and unseen felt thinner than breath.

The path wound through ancient woodland, the air damp with the scent of moss and wild earth. The sound of rushing water guided me forward, and as I approached the waterfall, I felt a shift a moment of stillness, as though the land itself was waiting for me to arrive.

St. Nectan's Glen has its own microclimate, where ferns grow thick along the banks and ancient trees stretch their gnarled limbs skyward, sheltering the sacred waters below. The air was heavy with moisture, carrying the scent of the earth, and the waters ran crystal clear, reflecting the emerald canopy above.

Drawn by an unspoken invitation, I stepped forward and waded into the shallows. The water was icy yet invigorating, wrapping around my ankles like a whispered blessing. Then, without hesitation, I stepped beneath the cascading waterfall, feeling its powerful flow wash over me, through me, into me. It was as if time itself had dissolved in the currents no past, no future, just this moment, just the sacred force of water in motion, cleansing, purifying, awakening.

As I stood beneath the waterfall, I lifted my hands to the sky and called in the directions, my voice weaving through the mist, carried by the wind, the water, and the unseen forces that had guided me here.

I turned to the East, feeling the cool breath of morning on my skin, whispering to the spirits of Air. "Bring me clarity, vision, and inspiration," I murmured, the leaves rustling in response.

I turned to the South, where the hidden sun infused the water with golden light. "Fill me with the fire of passion, courage, and transformation," I whispered, feeling the pulse of energy stir deep within.

I turned to the West, listening to the ceaseless flow of the waterfall, the sound mirroring the tides of my own emotions. "Teach me the wisdom of Water to surrender, to trust, and to let go," I said, my hands still submerged in its sacred currents.

I turned to the North, grounding my feet deeper into the cool, smooth stones beneath the water, feeling the steady presence of the earth. "Guide me with the wisdom of the ancestors, the strength of the land, and the patience of the great trees," I prayed, leaning into the embrace of the sacred Earth.

I stood in the centre of the mandala, the wheel of directions spinning around me, the elements alive, vibrant, present. And in that moment, I understood something profound:

This was a Remembering

A remembering of who I was before the world told me who to be. A remembering of the wisdom that had always lived in my bones. A remembering that the land is always listening and when we call upon the directions, they call back.

As I stepped out from beneath the falls, a single raven called overhead, its wings slicing through the grey sky, a final blessing from the unseen.

From that day forward, I knew that wherever I stood whether by a sacred well, within a stone circle, beneath an ancient oak, or at the edge of the ocean I carried the wisdom of the mandala directions within me. They were not just points on a compass. They were living forces of nature. Navigating the twists and turns of our lives can feel like trying to find our way through a dense fog. It's easy to feel disconnected, uncertain of where to turn, or even unsure of who we truly are.

Yet, as ancient cultures and mystical traditions have long understood, the four cardinal directions East, South, West, and

North are more than mere points on a map. These directions stand as eternal guides and guardians. They embody energies and archetypes that mirror the many dimensions of our lives and inner worlds.

When we align with these energies, they become an inner compass creating to navigate the path of self discovery and growth. When we tune into our inner compass and 'follow our true north' the directions can offer us guidance to find clarity, balance, and purpose, in our life. And when we listen, we find our way home.

That day beneath the waterfall was not just a ritual—it was a recalibration of my inner compass. It reminded me that sacred living is not found in perfection, but in alignment. The directions, once external guides marked on ancient stone and whispered through trees, had become inner archetypes, living within me. Each time I light a candle, call in the elements, or simply pause to breathe, I am re-entering the mandala. I am coming home to the sacred geometry of life itself.

THE MANDALA DIRECTIONS AND THEIR ENERGIES

Each direction holds its own unique energy, guiding us through different aspects of our journey, while the centre of the compass embodies the element of Ether or Spirit. This is the central point where all energies converge and from which all spiritual insights flow.

- **East (Air):** The direction of beginnings, inspiration, dawn and the dawning of new ideas. This is where we awaken, set our intentions, and connect with the breath of life. Morning rituals such as journaling, meditation, and goal-setting are particularly potent when aligned with the East,

as this direction helps ignite creativity and clarity.
- **South (Fire):** The direction of passion, action, the energy of noon. We are called to take bold steps towards our goals, ignite our inner fire, and embrace transformation. Practices such as dynamic yoga, dance, or any form of physical exercise are enhanced when oriented towards the South, as this direction fuels our motivation and courage.
- **West (Water):** The direction of introspection, emotions, and the setting sun. It is the place of healing, where we dive deep into our inner waters, release what no longer serves us, and connect with our intuition. Evening rituals such as reflective journaling, cleansing baths, or meditation are especially powerful when aligned with the West, as they help us process emotions and let go of the day.
- **North (Earth):** The direction of stability, wisdom, and the midnight hour. This is where we ground ourselves, connect with our ancestors, and find the strength to stand firm in our truth. Grounding practices such as walking in nature, sitting in stillness, or working with crystals, resonate deeply when aligned with the North, as this direction provides the stability and wisdom needed for profound spiritual work.
- **Centre (Ether/Spirit):** The direction of the practitioner, representing the element of Ether or Spirit. The centre is the focal point of the Mandala, embodying the unity of all directions and elements. As the element of Ether, the practitioner integrates and harmonises the energies of Air, Fire, Water, and Earth, holding the wisdom of the Mandala within. This central point is where all spiritual insights converge, the practitioner anchors the insights and energies for the entire mandala.

By consciously aligning our practices with these directions and recognising the practitioner as the central point, the bindu, embodying the element of Ether or Spirit we activate the

Mandala's full potential. This ensures that our journey through the Mandala is balanced, harmonious, and deeply connected to the wisdom held within the Mandala's sacred structure.

Chapter 11
East: New Beginnings

Each morning, as the kettle begins its soft boil, I open the French doors to let Luna out and step into the stillness of the day's first light. The air is fresh, full of promise. I inhale deeply the first sacred conscious breath and gaze toward the ancient trees that hold vigil at the edge of the garden.

Their changing form through the seasons reminds me that nothing stays the same, and that each day is a new invitation to begin again.

The East is where the Element of Air presides, symbolising new beginnings, inspiration and the breath of life. Spring, its corresponding season, reflects the awakening of potential, while dawn and the Waxing Moon phase amplify this energy, inviting us to grow and nurture our intentions. In the cycle of womanhood, the East corresponds to the Maiden, embodying youth, exploration, and blossoming potential.

Qualities of the East:
New Beginnings & Inspiration

The East is the direction of the rising sun — a place of fresh breath, clarity, and awakening. It carries the energy of new beginnings, where ideas are born and vision starts to take shape.

This is the realm of inspiration, where the winds of possibility whisper to the soul, stirring creativity and illuminating new pathways. In the East, we attune to the clarity of mind and the courage to begin again.

The East aligns with the Maiden phase in the cycle of womanhood, representing innocence, potential, curiosity, and the dawn of new possibilities.

- **Element:** Air
- **Season:** Spring
- **Time of Day:** Dawn
- **Lunar Cycle:** Waxing Moon
- **Phase of Womanhood:** Maiden

INSIGHTS FROM THE EAST

- **Embrace Change:** Like the dawn heralds a new day, the East encourages us to welcome change with an open heart and mind.
- **Seek Knowledge:** The element of Air invites us to expand our horizons by learning new things.
- **Express Yourself:** Use this time to communicate clearly and express your authentic self.
- **Reflect on New Starts:** Consider the new beginnings in your life.

JOURNALING PROMPTS FOR THE EAST

- **New Beginnings:** What new beginnings are you experiencing? How can you embrace these changes?
- **Inspiration and Creativity:** What inspires you? How can you channel this into creative projects?

- **Clarity and Communication:** In which areas do you need more clarity? How can you improve communication?
- **Planting Seeds:** What projects or intentions do you wish to nurture?
- **Embracing Change:** Reflect on a recent change. How did you handle it, and what did you learn?

AIR: RITUAL FOR CONNECTING WITH THE ELEMENT OF AIR

Purpose: To connect with the element of Air, cultivating clarity, inspiration, and communication.

Materials:
- A yellow or white candle (representing the element of Air)
- A feather or a piece of clear quartz
- Incense (such as sandalwood or frankincense) or sage for smudging
- A journal and pen

Steps:
- **Prepare Your Space:** Find a quiet space where you can sit comfortably. Place the candle, feather or crystal, and incense in front of you. Light the incense or sage for smudging.
- **Light the Candle:** Light the yellow or white candle to symbolise the element of Air and its qualities of clarity and inspiration.
- **Smudging Ritual:** Use the incense or sage to smudge yourself and your space, clearing any negative energy and inviting in the fresh, cleansing energy of Air.
- **Breathing and Centring:** Sit comfortably, close your eyes, and take several deep breaths. Focus on the sensation of air

filling your lungs, bringing clarity and lightness to your mind and body.
- **Invocation:** Hold the feather or clear quartz in your hand. Silently or aloud, invoke the presence of the element of Air and ask for clarity, inspiration, and clear communication.
- **Meditation:** Meditate for a few minutes, focusing on the qualities of Air its lightness, freedom, and movement. Visualise yourself being uplifted by a gentle breeze, clearing away mental fog and bringing fresh insights.
- **Closing:** Sit quietly for a few moments, feeling the lightness and clarity that Air brings. When you feel ready, extinguish the candle and give thanks for the guidance and inspiration.

Chapter 12
South: Passion and Transformation

At the height of the day, I often return to fire through movement perhaps a short, energising practice, dancing in the kitchen, a few rounds of breath of fire if I'm working in the therapy centre, or stepping outside to feel the sun warm my skin.

Fire is the element of sacred action, of showing up fully to life. I might light a candle, sip cacao, or drum to kindle up the energy and awaken the inner flame.

South is associated with the element of Fire, symbolising passion, transformation, and energy. This direction represents the spark of life, drive, and the power to create and transform. Fire reminds me of my purpose, my passion. It asks, where are you ready to act from the heart? Summer, the season of the South, is a time of growth, vitality, and abundance. Noon, its time of day, represents the peak of the sun's power. The cycle of the Full Moon signifies the fruition and manifestation of intentions.

The South aligns with the Mother phase in the cycle of womanhood, representing nurturing, creation, and the full bloom of life's potential.

South: Passion and Transformation

- **Element:** Fire
- **Season:** Summer
- **Time of Day:** Noon
- **Lunar Cycle:** Full Moon
- **Phase of Womanhood:** Mother

Qualities of the South: Vitality & Sacred Action

- **Passion:** The South ignites passion and drive, encouraging us to pursue our desires with enthusiasm and courage.
- **Transformation:** It is a time for transformation, where energy is harnessed to bring about change and growth.
- **Energy:** The South is about high energy, action, and vitality. It supports us in taking bold steps and embracing life fully.
- **Creativity:** This direction enhances creativity and the ability to bring ideas into reality. It's a time to innovate and express your inner fire.

Insights from the South

- **Ignite Your Passion:** Identify what truly excites you and focus your energy on pursuing it. Passion fuels progress and keeps you motivated.
- **Embrace Transformation:** Allow the energy of the South to transform areas of your life that need change. Be open to new experiences and growth.
- **Harness Your Energy:** Use the high energy of the South to take action on your goals. Don't hesitate; now is the time to move forward.
- **Express Your Creativity:** Channel your creative energy into projects and ideas that inspire you. The South supports

bringing your visions to life.

JOURNALING PROMPTS FOR THE SOUTH

- **Igniting Passion:** What are you passionate about? How can you incorporate more of this into your life?
- **Embracing Transformation:** Reflect on a significant change and its lessons.
- **Harnessing Energy:** Where do you need to act? What steps can you take towards your goals?

FIRE: RITUAL FOR CONNECTING WITH THE ELEMENT OF FIRE

Purpose: To connect with the element of Fire, igniting passion, transformation, and inner strength.

Materials:
- A red or orange candle (representing the element of Fire)
- A piece of citrine or carnelian
- Incense or sage for smudging
- A journal and pen

Steps:
- **Prepare Your Space:** Find a quiet space where you can sit comfortably. Place the candle, stone, and incense in front of you. Light the incense or sage for smudging.
- **Light the Candle:** Light the red or orange candle to symbolise the element of Fire and its qualities of passion and transformation.
- **Smudging Ritual:** Use the incense or sage to smudge yourself and your space, clearing any stagnant energy and

inviting in the vibrant, transformative energy of Fire.
- **Energising Meditation:** Sit comfortably, close your eyes, and take several deep breaths. Visualise a warm, glowing fire within you, igniting your passion and inner strength.
- **Invocation:** Hold the citrine or carnelian in your hand. Silently or aloud, invoke the presence of the element of Fire and ask for courage, passion, and the power to transform challenges into opportunities.
- **Meditation:** Meditate for a few minutes, focusing on the qualities of Fire its warmth, power, and transformative nature. Visualise yourself burning away any obstacles, leaving you renewed and energised.
- **Closing:** Sit quietly for a few moments, feeling the warmth and power of Fire within you. When you feel ready, extinguish the candle and give thanks for the courage and energy.

Chapter 13
West: Harvest and Reflection

As the sun starts to set at dusk, I turn to the element of water. At this time of day, I run a bath infused with salts, herbs, or rose petals and take a moment of space where I can soften the edges of the day and return to myself. Other times it's a shower of flowing water, letting the water wash away not just the physical debris, but any emotional weight I may be carrying. This is my time to listen to the heart, to the body, to what is rising from within.

The West is aligned with the element of Water, symbolising emotions, intuition, and healing. Water welcomes all of it the tears, the tenderness, the clarity. Water embodies the flow of life, adaptability, and the subconscious.

Dusk, it's time of day, marks the winding down of the day, while the Waning Moon represents a period of release, reflection, and renewal. Autumn, the season of the West, is a time of harvest, letting go, and preparing for rest.

The West corresponds with the Wild Woman phase, embodying maturity, reclaiming oneself, self-discovery, and embracing on adventures in life.

- **Element:** Water
- **Season:** Autumn.
- **Time of Day:** Dusk
- **Lunar Cycle:** Waning Moon
- **Phase of Womanhood:** Wild Woman

QUALITIES OF THE WEST

- **Intuition:** Enhances inner knowing and guidance.
- **Healing:** Focuses on emotional release and healing.
- **Flow:** Emphasises adaptability and acceptance.
- **Reflection:** Encourages introspection and preparation for renewal.

INSIGHTS FROM THE WEST

- **Trust Your Intuition:** Follow your inner voice and gut feelings.
- **Heal Emotionally:** Release past wounds and practise forgiveness.
- **Surrender:** Water teaches us how to feel deeply, and how to surrender to the flow.
- **Go with the Flow:** Embrace life's natural rhythm and adapt to changes.
- **Reflect on Achievements:** Consider what you've accomplished and what needs to be let go.

JOURNALING PROMPTS FOR THE WEST

- **Trusting Intuition:** When has your intuition guided you effectively? How can you strengthen this connection?
- **Emotional Healing:** What wounds need healing? How can you begin this process?
- **Going with the Flow:** Where do you resist change? How can you flow more naturally?
- **Reflecting on Achievements:** List your achievements and the lessons learned from them.

WATER: RITUAL FOR CONNECTING WITH THE ELEMENT OF WATER

Purpose: To connect with Water, promoting emotional healing and intuition.

Materials:
- Blue or white candle
- bowl of water or seashell
- moonstone or aquamarine
- journal and pen.

Steps:
- **Prepare Your Space:** Find a quiet space where you can sit comfortably. Place the candle, bowl of water or seashell, and stone in front of you.
- **Light the Candle:** Light the blue or white candle to symbolise the element of Water and its qualities of emotional depth and intuition.
- **Smudging Ritual:** Smudge yourself and your space with incense or sage, if desired, inviting the soothing and cleans-

ing energy of Water.
- **Flowing Meditation:** Sit comfortably, close your eyes, and take several deep breaths. Visualise a gentle stream or the ebb and flow of the ocean, bringing calm and emotional healing.
- **Invocation:** Hold the moonstone or aquamarine in your hand. Silently or aloud, invoke the presence of the element of Water and ask for emotional balance, intuition, and ease of flow in your life.
- **Meditation:** Meditate for a few minutes, focusing on the qualities of Water its fluidity, depth, and soothing nature. Visualise any emotional blockages dissolving in the gentle flow of water.
- **Closing:** Sit quietly for a few moments, feeling the calm and healing energy of Water. When you feel ready, extinguish the candle and give thanks for the emotional clarity and balance.

Chapter 14

North: Reflection and Renewal

There is a moment, often in the quiet at the end of the day, when I step barefoot onto the earth beside the yurt the place where so many circles were once held. The soil beneath me is steady, cool, alive. Sometimes I sit with a warm drink in silence, or place my hands on the earth to listen, to root, to remember.

Earth holds the memory of all that has come before. It asks nothing of me but presence. This is where I come to restore, to listen to the ancestors, and to return to what is true beneath the noise.

"In stillness, the roots speak. In silence, we remember."

The North is connected to the element of Earth, symbolising stability, grounding, and physicality. Earth represents nourishment, growth, and the material world. Winter, the season of the North, is a time of rest, reflection, and inner work. By embracing patience we understand that growth often requires patience and perseverance. Trust in the process and the cycles of life.

Midnight, its time of day, represents deep rest and introspection. The lunar phase of New Moon is the darkest phase of the moon but it signifies a fresh start filled with potential.

By exploring each direction, we align ourselves with the natural cycles and elemental energies that shape our lives. Embrace the wisdom of the East, South, West, and North as they guide you

through a journey of growth, passion, reflection, and renewal. Your inner compass, shaped by these directions, will lead you towards a more harmonious and fulfilling existence.

The North aligns with the Wise Woman phase, representing wisdom, experience, reflection, and the culmination of life's experiences.

- **Element:** Earth
- **Season:** Winter
- **Time of Day:** Midnight
- **Lunar Cycle:** New Moon
- **Phase of Womanhood:** Wise Woman

QUALITIES OF THE NORTH

- **Grounding:** The North provides stability and grounding energy.
- **Reflection:** It is a time for introspection and contemplation.
- **Nourishment:** Focus on self-care and nurturing the body.
- **Persistence:** The North teaches patience and perseverance through challenging times.

INSIGHTS FROM THE NORTH

- **Ground Yourself:** Connect with the earth through grounding practices like walking barefoot, gardening, or meditating in nature.
- **Reflect Deeply:** Use the stillness of winter to reflect on your journey, reassess your goals, and plans.

- **Nourish Your Body:** Pay attention to your physical well being. Eat nourishing foods, rest adequately, and care for your body.

JOURNALING PROMPTS FOR THE NORTH

- **Grounding Practices:** What activities help you feel grounded and connected to the earth? How can you incorporate more grounding practices into your daily routine?
- **Deep Reflection:** Reflect on your journey over the past year. What were the key lessons learned? How can you use these lessons to shape your future?
- **Nourishing the Body:** What steps can you take to nourish your body, mind, and spirit? Create a self-care plan that includes physical, mental, and spiritual nourishment.
- **Embracing Patience:** Reflect on a time when patience was essential in your life. What did you learn from that experience? How can you cultivate more patience and perseverance in your current endeavours?

EARTH: RITUAL FOR CONNECTING WITH THE ELEMENT OF EARTH

Purpose: Connect with the Earth, cultivating grounding, stability, and nourishment.

Materials:
- A green or brown candle (representing the element of Earth)
- A piece of hematite or black tourmaline

- A bowl of soil or sand
- A journal and pen

Steps:
- **Prepare Your Space:** Find a quiet space where you can sit comfortably. Place the candle, stone, and bowl of soil or sand in front of you.
- **Light the Candle:** Light the green or brown candle to symbolise the element of Earth and its qualities of grounding and nourishment.
- **Smudging Ritual:** Smudge yourself and your space with incense or sage, inviting the stable and nurturing energy of Earth.
- **Grounding Meditation:** Sit comfortably, close your eyes, and take several deep breaths. Visualise roots growing from your body into the earth, grounding and stabilising you.
- **Invocation:** Hold the hematite or black tourmaline in your hand. Silently or aloud, invoke the presence of the element of Earth and ask for grounding, stability, and the strength to support your endeavours.
- **Meditation:** Meditate for a few minutes, focusing on the qualities of Earth its strength, stability, and nurturing nature. Visualise yourself being nourished and supported by the earth beneath you.
- **Closing:** Sit quietly for a few moments, feeling the grounding and supportive energy of Earth. When you feel ready, extinguish the candle and give thanks for the stability and nourishment.

Chapter 15

Ether: Great Spirit Connecting As Above, So Below

In the quiet space between moments, before the breath, between the heartbeat, there is Ether. It is the space that holds everything and nothing. Sometimes I meet it in meditation, when the edges blur and I feel part of something vast and luminous. Other times, it's in the pause between words in circle, or the silence that follows a prayer.

Ether is not something we do, but something we allow. It reminds me that beyond the physical, beyond even the elements, there is the essence of spirit, always present, always listening. Ether is the sacred space where everything belongs. It is the breath behind the breath, the silence beneath the song.

This element embodies the unity of all directions and the integration of all phases of life. The Great Spirit Ether transcends the limitations of time and the cycles of nature, representing the eternal and infinite presence that is always available to us.

The Great Spirit represents the essence that binds all phases and experiences together, reminding us of the interconnectedness of all life.

- **Element:** Spirit (Ether)
- **Time of Day:** All Times Lunar
- **Cycle:** All Cycles
- **Phase of Womanhood:** Integration of Experience
- **Cycle of Life:** Unity and Wholeness.

QUALITIES OF THE GREAT SPIRIT

- **Unity:** The Great Spirit embodies the interconnectedness of all things, reminding us that every element of existence is linked. It invites us to see beyond duality and embrace the oneness of life.
- **Divine Connection:** This element represents the bridge between the physical and the divine. It encourages the nurturing of our relationship with the higher power, understanding that we are both physical beings and spiritual entities.
- **Wholeness:** Wholeness is about integrating all aspects of ourselves, light and shadow, joy and sorrow, strength and vulnerability. The Great Spirit helps us embrace our entire being without judgement.
- **Alignment:** The Great Spirit calls us to align our spiritual and physical selves. It urges us to live in harmony with our deepest values and truths, ensuring that our actions are in sync with our spiritual purpose.

INSIGHTS FROM THE GREAT SPIRIT

- **Recognise the Divine in All Things:** The Great Spirit teaches us to see the sacred in every experience and being, honouring a sense of reverence and gratitude for all of life.
- **Align Your Spiritual and Physical Selves:** This insight emphasises the importance of balancing our spiritual

aspirations with our daily actions. When our inner and outer worlds align, we live more authentically and with greater integrity.
- **Embrace Unity and Wholeness:** The Great Spirit reminds us that we are part of a larger whole. By embracing unity, we cultivate a sense of belonging and community, and by accepting all parts of ourselves, we achieve true wholeness.
- **Seek Divine Guidance:** Connecting with the Great Spirit allows us to access wisdom and guidance from the divine. This connection can illuminate our path, offering clarity and support in times of need.

JOURNALING PROMPTS FOR THE GREAT SPIRIT

- **Connection Between Spiritual and Physical Selves:** How do you experience the connection between your spiritual and physical selves? Reflect on moments when you felt a strong connection between your body and spirit. Describe these experiences and what they mean to you.
- **Practices for Divine Connection:** What practices help you feel aligned with the divine? Identify and describe the activities or rituals that enhance your connection to the divine. How do these practices impact your daily life?
- **Experiencing Unity and Wholeness:** Reflect on a moment when you felt a deep sense of unity and wholeness. What contributed to that feeling? Think about a specific time when you felt complete and unified. What were the circumstances, and how did this experience shape your perspective?
- **Inviting Divine Guidance:** How can you invite more divine guidance and wisdom into your daily life? Explore ways to integrate spiritual practices into your routine. Consider meditation, prayer, or other activities that open you to divine insights.

GREAT SPIRIT: RITUAL FOR CONNECTING AS ABOVE, SO BELOW

Purpose: To connect with the divine, aligning the spiritual (above) with the physical (below).

Materials:
- A white candle (representing divine light)
- A piece of selenite or any high-vibration stone
- Incense or sage for smudging
- A journal and pen

Steps:
- **Prepare Your Space:** Find a quiet space where you can sit comfortably. Place the candle, stone, and incense in front of you. Light the incense or sage for smudging.
- **Light the Candle:** Light the white candle to symbolise the divine light and connection to the Great Spirit.
- **Smudging Ritual:** Use the incense or sage to smudge yourself and your space, clearing any negative energy and inviting in divine presence.
- **Grounding and Centring:** Sit comfortably, close your eyes, and take several deep breaths. Imagine a beam of light connecting you from the top of your head (crown chakra) to the earth beneath you (root chakra), aligning you with the energies above and below.
- **Invocation:** Hold the selenite crystal in your hand. Silently or aloud, invoke the presence of the Great Spirit and ask for guidance, protection, and alignment in your life.
- **Meditation:** Meditate for a few minutes, focusing on the connection between the divine and the physical, the "As Above, So Below." Visualise this alignment, bringing harmony and balance into your life.
- **Closing the Ritual:** Sit quietly for a few moments, feeling

the connection between the spiritual and physical. When you feel ready, extinguish the candle and give thanks for the guidance and alignment.

PART III
EMBODYING THE MYSTIC WITHIN

CHAPTER 16
THE POWER OF INVOCATION

The deep, resonant sound of a temple bell echoed through the early morning air. The scent of incense curled in delicate tendrils towards the sky, mingling with the stillness before dawn. Wrapped in the hush of the sacred moment, I closed my eyes, my breath steady, my heart open.

The temple, nestled in the foothills of the Himalayas, was bathed in the golden glow of flickering oil lamps, and as the first chant of invocation rose, a wave of reverence passed through me. This was a calling a summoning of the divine, a bridge between realms, an invitation to the sacred.

DEEPENING OUR CONNECTION

An invocation is a sacred call, a way to invite divine energies, spiritual guides, or higher consciousness into our lives. In spiritual practices, invocations are a powerful way to create a bridge between the material and spiritual realms, opening channels for guidance, healing, and transformation.

As we invoke, we enter a sacred dialogue with the universe, inviting divine assistance into our lives. With sincere intention, reverence, and gratitude, invocations can become an integral part of your spiritual journey, enhancing your sacred living and guiding you toward your deepest wisdom.

The Power of Invocation

Invocations are potent tools for deepening our connection to the divine and opening ourselves to higher wisdom. Whether used in ritual, meditation, or daily practice, they help to align our energies with our highest intentions.

Invocations Calling upon the Divine

Rooted in ancient wisdom and used across various traditions, invocations allow us to call upon the divine to assist in our journey, clarify our purpose, and deepen our connection to the mysteries of the universe.

An invocation acts as a channel, allowing us to attune ourselves to a particular energy or intention. The act of speaking an invocation with an open heart and focused mind sends out a call to the universe, inviting that energy into your life. It is an energetic exchange when you invoke the divine, you create an opening for transformation, healing, or insight.

How to Invoke with Intention

The essence of any invocation is intention. Whether you are invoking for guidance, protection, healing, or creativity, the words you speak have energy. When spoken with sincerity and devotion, invocations have the power to align us with higher consciousness, opening us to divine support and wisdom.

Invocations are particularly powerful when used to create sacred space, whether at the beginning of a ritual, before meditation, or during a personal moment of reflection. They allow you to consciously connect with a higher power, shift the energy around you, and set a clear direction for your spiritual journey.

- **Set Your Intention** – Before you begin, pause and reflect on your intention. What is your purpose in invoking? Are you calling for clarity, healing, or divine guidance? By clarifying your intention, you can better align the energy of your invocation to the specific outcome you desire.
- **Create Sacred Space** – Establish a peaceful, sacred environment where you can focus your energy. You might light a candle, burn incense, or place an object with spiritual significance before you. Creating an atmosphere that feels sacred invites the presence of divine energy and clears away distractions.
- **Speak with Reverence** – Invocations are an act of reverence and humility. Approach them with respect for the divine energies you are calling upon. Whether you are invoking a higher power, a spiritual guide, or your own inner wisdom, speak the words with intention and honour.
- **Feel the Energy** – As you speak your invocation, allow yourself to feel the energy of the words you are using. Visualise the divine energy you are calling upon filling the space, enveloping you, and guiding you. Trust that as you speak, you are creating a powerful energetic shift.
- **Close with Gratitude** – When you have completed your invocation, always express gratitude. Give thanks for the divine assistance, clarity, or guidance that has been offered. Gratitude seals the energy and makes space for the divine to work in your life.

To Create Your Own Invocation

- **State your purpose:** What do you seek in this invocation? For example, Clarity, healing, protection, inspiration.
- **Invite the energy:** Name the divine force, archetype, or essence you are calling upon (eg. Divine Wisdom, Sacred Feminine, etc.)
- **Ask for assistance:** Clearly state what you would like the energy or force to help you with.
- **Express gratitude:** Always close with a thank you, knowing that the divine has heard your call and will respond in perfect timing.

The Role of Sound and Voice in Invocations

In many spiritual traditions, sound is a vital tool for invoking higher energies. Mantras, chants, and singing bowls have long been used to raise vibration and strengthen intention. When performing an invocation, the tone and cadence of your voice shape its energy, amplifying the resonance of your words.

You may be called to repeat an invocation multiple times, allowing the vibrations to deepen within you. Repetition not only reinforces the sacred intention but also brings a meditative quality to the practice. In the yoga tradition, for example, mantras are often chanted 108 times a number believed to hold spiritual significance, representing wholeness and connection to the divine. Repetition can help focus the mind, harmonise your energy, and strengthen the invocation's potency.

Vocalising with Flow

Experimenting with vocalisation can enhance your invocation practice. Rather than speaking in a monotone, allow your voice to flow naturally rising and falling in a way that feels organic and resonant. This rhythmic approach can create a deeper energetic connection, helping you open more fully to divine presence and guidance.

Invocations for a Purpose

Divine Wisdom

"I call upon the sacred wisdom that resides within me and within the universe. May the light of divine insight guide me on my path.

"With open heart and mind, I invite wisdom to flow through me, to reveal the truth of my soul's purpose. I surrender to the flow of divine guidance, trusting that all I need will be revealed in perfect timing. Blessed be."

Sacred Feminine

"Great Divine Feminine, She who flows through all life, I call upon your nurturing, wisdom, and power. May your love fill my heart and awaken my intuition.

Grant me the strength to walk in my truth, the grace to embody your divine presence, and the courage to stand in my power. As the rose blooms, so too may my heart open to the gifts of your sacred love. Blessed be."

CLARITY AND GUIDANCE

"I invoke the energies of clarity and divine insight. May the fog of confusion lift, and may the path ahead be illuminated by the light of truth. Guide me in making wise decisions and seeing the world through the eyes of love and understanding.

"I open myself to receive the guidance I need, trusting in the wisdom of the universe to lead me to my highest good. Blessed be."

EARTH

"Great Earth, our sacred mother, I call upon your grounding energy and your nurturing spirit. May I be deeply connected to your energies, drawing strength from your roots and wisdom from your embrace.

"Help me to walk lightly on this earth, with reverence for all living beings. May I remember that I am part of the web of life, interconnected with all that is. Blessed be."

HEALING

"I call upon the healing light of the Divine to enter my body, mind, and spirit. I open myself to receive the transformative energy of love and compassion. May all wounds, physical, emotional, and spiritual, be healed by the sacred light that surrounds me. May I be restored to my highest state of well-being, whole and complete in body, heart, and soul. Blessed be."

DIVINE MASCULINE

"Great Divine Masculine, protector and creator, I call upon your strength and clarity. May your wisdom guide my actions and decisions, empowering me to live with purpose and integrity. Help me to embody the courage and resilience needed to face life's challenges with grace. May your protective energy surround me, keeping me steady as I walk my path. Blessed be."

Chapter 17
Invocations for Sacred Ceremony

Sacred Mandala Ceremony: Invocation to the Directions

Begin by standing or sitting in a quiet, sacred space to connect deeply with the energies you wish to invoke. Place your hands in prayer position at your heart or extend them outward in a gesture of receptivity.

Divine Source of All Wisdom, Guardians of the Sacred Mandala, We gather here in reverence, To honour the ancient and infinite knowledge, That flows through the very fabric of existence.

As we stand at the threshold of this sacred practice, we call upon the four directions: the elements, the guardians, and the wisdom keepers, to encircle us with their protection, guide us with their light, and fill our hearts with the clarity of truth.

In the East, we invoke the powers of Inspiration and Awakening, The realm of new beginnings and enlightenment. We call upon the sacred fires of the East to ignite the spark of divine insight within us and illuminate the darkness of our understanding so that we may rise with the dawn of greater awareness.

In the South, we invoke the powers of Transformation and Power, The realm of action and growth. We call upon the sacred flames of the South to burn away all that no longer serves us and empower us with the strength and courage to embrace change and manifest our true potential.

In the West, we invoke the powers of Intuition and Reflection, The realm of emotions and the inner world. We call upon the sacred waters of the West to cleanse and heal our hearts and deepen our connection with our inner wisdom so that we may flow with the currents of divine guidance.

In the North, we invoke the powers of Wisdom and Clarity, The realm of the mind and higher knowledge. We call upon the sacred winds of the North, to sweep away all confusion and doubt,

And to bring us the clear vision of our path, That we may walk it with purpose and precision.

At the Centre of the Mandala, we invoke the essence of Unity and Wholeness. The space where all directions converge and all wisdom is one. We call upon the sacred Earth beneath us, A symbol of stability and grounding, To ground us in the present moment and support us as we journey within, To the core of our being, to the heart of the Mandala.

Great Spirit, Divine Wisdom, Eternal Light, We ask that you bless this sacred practice, That our hearts may be open, our minds clear, And our spirits aligned with the highest truth.

May the Mandala of Wisdom reveal to us, The path we are meant to walk, The lessons we are meant to learn, And the divine essence that resides within us all.

With gratitude and humility, We dedicate this practice, To the unfolding of wisdom, To the awakening of consciousness, And to the service of all beings, across all times and dimensions.

So it is. So it shall be.

End the invocation by bringing your hands to your heart in gratitude or bowing to acknowledge the energies you have called upon.

MANDALA OF WISDOM INVOCATION

Sacred Ones ...

We call upon the energies of the four directions,
The whispering winds of the East,
The great flame of the South,
The eternal healing waters of the West, The fertile earth of the North,
The As Above and So Below ...
And Great Spirit to dance freely in our bodies, minds, hearts, and souls. Ancestors, guides, ascended beings, be with us today for our healing, growth, and transformation.
We ask that anything that is released today be drawn down into the Earth
through the power of the sacred vortex
To be transmuted and transformed.
We ask that everything be in accordance with universal law,
Honouring the divine feminine, sacred masculine, and may no one harm the children.
Blessed Be, Aho, Awen, Amen, Namaste ...

INVOCATION FOR A DAILY PRACTICE
Opening Invocation

Begin by standing or sitting quietly, with hands in prayer position or placed over your heart.

Divine light within and around me, I call upon your presence as I begin this sacred practice. May wisdom, clarity, and love guide my

thoughts and actions today. I open my heart to this moment's teachings and align myself with the highest truth.
So it is.

Closing Invocation

End by bringing your hands to your heart or bowing slightly.

With gratitude, I close this sacred practice. May the insights and peace I have received, Carry me forward with grace and purpose. I honour the divine within and around me.
So it is.

BEGINNING A MOVEMENT PRACTICE

Step onto your mat with the intention of embodying the principles of balance and unity. Start with a grounding exercise to centre yourself. Stand with your feet hip-width apart, arms at your sides, and take a few deep breaths. Feel the connection of your feet to the Earth, grounding yourself in the present moment.

SUN WISE MOVEMENTS

Begin moving sun wise, following the path of the sun to the right. As you do, invoke the energies of the sun and the sacred masculine. Perform each posture with intention, embracing action and strength. Let your movements be bold and purposeful, reflecting the outward expression of creative force.

MOON WISE MOVEMENTS

Transition to moon wise movements, moving to the left, aligning with the Moon and the divine feminine. Embrace the qualities of intuition, reflection, and nurturing. Move with grace and fluidity, allowing your movements to flow and respond to your inner rhythm.

Engaging the Elements

As you move through the directions, engage with the elements. Visualise each element not just as external forces but as integral parts of your being: Air as your breath, Fire as your passion, Water as your emotions, and Earth as your physical presence. This integration deepens the practice, making it both internal and external. Face East to breathe in the energy of Air, welcoming new beginnings. Move South to connect with Fire, embracing transformation. Turn West to invite the flow of Water, delving into introspection. Face North to draw in the stability and wisdom of Earth.

Reflection and Integration

Conclude your practice by opening your arms wide, honouring the Star and the Cosmos. Feel your profound connection to the infinite and the mysterious. Recognise your place in the universe and open yourself to the wisdom and possibilities that lie beyond.

Take a moment to sit in stillness, reflecting on the experience. Journaling any insights, emotions, or sensations that emerged during the practice, making a note of its lessons as they become tangible in your daily life. This reflection helps ground the experience. Integrate the insights and energies you have encountered, allowing them to inform your journey moving forward. The Mandala of Wisdom is more than a physical practice; it is a sacred journey towards inner balance and cosmic unity. As you step off your mat, carry the essence of the Mandala with you, allowing it to guide your daily life and deepen your connection with the world around you.

LIVING WITHIN THE MANDALA

The Mandala of Wisdom is not confined to the altar, the mat, or even the moment of ritual—it lives within you. Each time you call in the directions, move in reverence, or speak an invocation from the heart, you activate this sacred geometry within your own being. The elements are not separate from you; they are your breath, your blood, your fire, your bones. When you move through the world with presence and intention, you carry the temple with you. You *are* the Mandala. Let this knowing anchor you as you navigate life's spirals—returning always to centre, to Spirit, to self. From this place, every act becomes sacred, and every moment an opportunity to remember who you truly are.

Chapter 18
The Divine Feminine and Sacred Masculine

In the sacred dance of the cosmos, two primordial forces weave the fabric of existence: Divine Feminine and the Sacred Masculine. These energies, ancient and eternal, form the essence of creation. They are not bound by gender or form but flow through all things, infusing the universe with balance, harmony, and life. Together, they create the vibrant tapestry of existence, Divine Feminine as the creative flow of life, like a river, and Sacred Masculine as the vessel, the archetype that provides structure, like the banks of the river. Understanding and honouring these energies within ourselves is a fundamental aspect of spiritual practice. Through this understanding, we come to know the fullness of our being, and through their union, we touch the heart of the divine.

In the sacred marriage of the Divine Feminine and the Sacred Masculine, a third energy is born. This third energy, often referred to as the Divine Union. This profound synergy represents love, creativity, and spiritual awakening, holding the key to our evolution as spiritual beings.

The Divine Feminine:
The Creative Flow of the River

The Divine Feminine is the wellspring of life, the nurturing force that sustains and nourishes all beings. This energy is like a river, a flowing, dynamic force that moves gracefully and with purpose, carving paths, shaping landscapes, and giving life to everything in its path.

This river is not confined to one form; it is ever changing, adapting to the contours of the land and reflecting the cycles of nature the ebb and flow of the tides, the waxing and waning of the moon, and the birth and death of the seasons. It carries the potential of all creation, the seeds of new life, ideas, and expressions waiting to emerge.

In yogic tradition, this energy is represented by Shakti and symbolised by the colour red the root chakra, the base of our energetic being, the point from which life flows. Red speaks to vitality, passion, and embodiment. It is both primal and sacred.

To connect with the Divine Feminine is to surrender to the movement of life. It is to release control and honour emotion as sacred data. This energy invites us into depth into the knowing that can't be found in books, only in stillness, dreams, and the womb-like dark. It teaches us to trust not what we think, but what we feel and sense.

THE SACRED MASCULINE: THE VESSEL, THE BANKS OF THE RIVER

While the Divine Feminine is the river, the Sacred Masculine is the banks that contain and guide this flow. The Sacred Masculine is the vessel, the structure and order that provides form and direction, ensuring that the creative energy of the Divine Feminine is channelled and utilised in a way that brings life into being.

The Sacred Masculine is the energy of action, structure, and purpose. It is the force that brings order to the creative chaos of the river. Just as the banks of a river shape its course, the Sacred

Masculine provides the boundaries and frameworks that allow the Divine Feminine to express its full potential. This energy is linear and focused, driving the forward movement of creation with intention and clarity.

In the yogic tradition, the Sacred Masculine energy is represented by the colour white a symbol of purity, clarity, and Shiva's expansive nature. White is associated with the crown chakra, representing the infinite, unchanging consciousness that underlies all of existence. It embodies stillness and spaciousness, the essence of the Sacred Masculine that holds and protects the flow of life.

To connect with the Sacred Masculine is to connect with the power of discipline, will, and direction. This energy teaches us the value of boundaries, the importance of honouring commitments, and the necessity of standing in our power. The voice of the Sacred Masculine is one of reason, guiding us with logic and strategy, helping us to manifest our dreams and bring our visions into reality.

The Sacred Masculine, its ability to provide a stable and secure foundation for the creative flow of life. The force holds space for the Divine Feminine, allowing it to flow wild and freely within a safe and supportive container.

THE SACRED UNION:
THE DANCE OF THE RIVER AND ITS RIVERBANKS

When the Divine Feminine and Sacred Masculine come together, they create a sacred union that embodies divine love and creative power. This union is not merely a merging of energies but a dynamic dance, where each energy honours and amplifies the other. The river flows freely within the boundaries set by the banks, and the banks are shaped and softened by the flow of the river. Together, they create a harmonious balance that allows life to thrive.

This energy is deeply creative and transformative. The union of the Divine Feminine and Sacred Masculine gives birth to new possibilities, ideas, and realities. It is the source of all creation, from the smallest act of kindness to the grandest vision of change. In this sacred space, we become co creators with the divine, manifesting our soul's purpose and contributing to the evolution of consciousness.

The sacred union also heals the wounds of separation, dissolving the barriers that isolate us from ourselves, divide us from each other, and separate us from the divine. In this embrace, we experience a profound sense of wholeness and unity, awakening the sacred potential within us.

SACRED WATERS OF
THE CHALICE WELL AND THE WHITE SPRING

This sacred union is beautifully exemplified in the landscape of Glastonbury at the Chalice Well, where two sacred springs flow side by side, each embodying the unique vibrations of the Divine Feminine and Sacred Masculine. These sacred springs known as the Red Spring and the White Spring, are potent symbols of these cosmic forces, offering a tangible experience of their balance and harmony.

Chalice Well with its red, iron rich waters, represents the Divine Feminine. It is a source of nurturing, healing, and the deep, intuitive wisdom that flows from the heart of the earth. The red water, symbolic of the life giving blood of the earth, invites those who visit to immerse themselves in the flow of life, to drink deeply from the well of feminine wisdom, and to honour the cycles of creation, destruction, and rebirth.

The White Spring nearby runs with clear, pure waters. This sacred spring embodies the Sacred Masculine. It is a place of protection, clarity, and the stillness that allows for deep contemplation and connection with the divine. The clear water of the White Spring represents the purifying aspects of the Sacred Masculine, a space where the mind can rest and the spirit can connect with the infinite.

Although the White Spring is typically associated with the Sacred Masculine, my own personal experience there revealed these energies' fluid nature. Standing before the crystal-clear waters, I felt a profound connection to the Divine Feminine, as a deep, nurturing presence that flowed through me like the softest whisper of the river.

This connection serves as a powerful reminder that rigid definitions do not confine these energies; they are beyond gender, transcending physical form, and they are open to our personal experiences and interpretation. Just as the banks of a river can shape the flow, so too can our understanding shape the energies we experience.

The close proximity of these two springs reflect the sacred union of the Divine Feminine and Sacred Masculine. The red waters of the Chalice Well and the white waters of the White Spring are like the yin and yang of life, each essential to the other, each enhancing the other's qualities. Together, they create a sacred space where the flow of life and the structure of consciousness meet, offering a profound experience of unity and wholeness.

Visitors to these springs are invited to drink from the healing waters of the Chalice Well, and purify themselves in the clear waters of the White Spring to experience both energies and integrate these energies within themselves, finding a balance between the nurturing, creative flow of the feminine and the protective, grounding structure of the masculine.

This integration of energies is a reflection of the greater cosmic dance, where the Divine Feminine and Sacred Masculine come together to create the beauty, harmony, and balance of the universe. As we connect with these sacred waters, we are reminded of our own potential to embody this balance, to live in harmony with the flow of life while maintaining the structure and clarity needed to manifest our highest purpose.

GUIDED VISUALISATION: THE SACRED UNION WITHIN

- **Find Your Space:** Sit comfortably in a quiet place. Close your eyes and take three deep breaths, inhaling through your nose and exhaling through your mouth.
- **Imagine the River:** Visualise a flowing river of vibrant red water. Feel its nurturing energy as it flows through you, awakening your intuition and creativity.
- **See the Banks:** Picture white, strong banks forming around the river, providing structure and direction. Sense their protective and grounding energy.
- **Feel the Dance:** Watch as the river flows within the banks, the two energies merging harmoniously. Notice how they support and enhance each other, creating a dynamic balance.
- **Embody the Union:** Feel the union of these energies within you the creative flow of the Divine Feminine and the stabilising force of the Sacred Masculine. Sit with this energy, allowing it to expand and fill your being.
- **Return to the Present:** Take three more deep breaths, bringing this balance into your heart and mind. Open your

eyes, feeling grounded and inspired.

REFLECTION

- In what areas of your life does your Divine Feminine express itself?
- Where does your Sacred Masculine offer strength or need tending?
- How do you experience balance and where might more harmony serve you?

EMBRACING THE SACRED UNION: A PATH TO WHOLENESS

To embrace the sacred union of the Divine Feminine and Sacred Masculine within oneself is to embark on a journey of deep spiritual growth and transformation. This path requires us to honour and integrate both energies within our being, recognising that they are not opposites but complementary forces that create the fullness of who we are.

We can cultivate this sacred union through daily spiritual practices that honour both the Divine Feminine and Sacred Masculine. Through meditation, we connect with the stillness of the Sacred Masculine, finding clarity and focus. Through prayer, we open to the wisdom of the Divine Feminine, receiving guidance and inspiration. Rituals create a sacred space where these energies can come together in harmony, cultivating a deeper connection with the divine. As we walk this path, we begin to see the Divine Feminine and Sacred Masculine as energies within us, and as forces at work in the world.

This recognition of balance and harmony becomes essential in all aspects of our life in our relationships, communities, and the broader environment. The journey becomes one of stewardship, where the sacred balance is nurtured, bringing healing and wholeness to the world.

Ultimately, the sacred union of the Divine Feminine and Sacred Masculine is not merely a personal journey; it is a cosmic one. It is a journey that leads to the heart of the divine, where unity with all that is becomes the guiding principle. In this union lies the deepest truth of existence that we are the creators of our reality, the stewards of the earth, and the living embodiment of the divine.

Chapter 19

The Hero's Journey and Shero's Journey

Embarking on the Sacred Path

In the vast, intricate tapestry of the human spirit, few narratives resonate as deeply and universally as the Hero's Journey. This archetypal odyssey, articulated with profound insight by Joseph Campbell, reflects not only the external adventures of mythic figures but also the inner quest for self realisation and spiritual awakening that resides within each of us. It is a journey of transformation, where we are called to transcend the familiar, confront the unknown, and return home with the elixir of wisdom a spiritual reward representing the deep insights and understanding gained from the challenges and trials of the Journey.

For me, the call to embark on this sacred path came unexpectedly. I had been working as a holistic therapist and spiritual healer for over 12 years, deeply committed to helping others on their journeys. Yet, a yearning began to stir within me, a sense that there was something more I was meant to do. Inspired by Deepak Chopra's books, I felt a pull to join a week-long meditation program, Seduction of Spirit.

In 2008, I packed my bags, kissed my young children and husband goodbye, and took a leap of faith. There was a deep call one I didn't fully understand at the time but I knew it was time to go deeper on my spiritual path. Joining a group of 500 people in

Dublin, I sat in the presence of Deepak Chopra, Dr. David Simon, and Davidji, allowing their teachings to guide me.

That week was a catalyst. It awakened something profound within me, creating a pathway I was destined to walk a path not only as a healer but as a teacher. By the end of the program, I had enrolled in my first spiritual teacher training 'Primordial Sound Meditation' with the Chopra Center, ready to step into a new chapter of my life. This moment marked the beginning of my Hero's Journey, the first step into the unknown, where I would face challenges, embrace transformation, and ultimately discover the deeper purpose that awaited me.

In this age of spiritual renaissance, we recognise that the Hero's Journey is one thread in the rich fabric of human experience. Complementing it is the Shero's Journey a path honouring the sacred feminine within us all. The Shero's Journey is a deeply introspective and cyclical pilgrimage that offers a counterbalance to the Hero's quest, reminding us of the power of nurturing, intuition, and the eternal cycles of life and death. Together, these journeys create a holistic map for the soul's evolution, guiding us through the trials and triumphs that shape our spiritual landscape. They are not merely stories to be admired from afar but living, breathing pathways that we each walk uniquely. The Hero's Journey, with its focus on external challenges, and the Shero's Journey, with its inner journey of healing, are not separate paths, they are complementary aspects of the same spiritual growth. To understand them is to understand the sacred rhythms of our existence; to engage with them is to embark on the most profound of spiritual practices.

The Hero's Journey:
A Sacred Quest for the Eternal Truth

The Hero's Journey begins with an invitation a call that stirs the soul from the sleepwalking of the ordinary world. This call often comes in the form of a crisis, a deep yearning, or an unexpected event that disrupts the comfort of routine. It is a moment of divine discontent where the soul recognises that there is something beyond the material world, something more waiting to be discovered. Answering this call requires immense courage, for it demands that we abandon the known and embrace the unknown to follow the calling.

To answer this call is to step across the threshold into the liminal space of adventure, where the rules of the old world no longer apply. In this sacred space, the Hero is stripped of their former identity, embarking on a path of profound transformation.

The trials that follow are not merely external challenges but these mirror reflections of the Hero's inner landscape. Each monster that is faced, each obstacle that we overcome, mirrors the Hero's inner demons, fears, and doubts. These trials and challenges are alchemical in nature, transforming the Hero at every stage of the Journey. They forge our strength, cultivate our wisdom, and ignite the flame of self-awareness. Through these crucibles of transformation, the Hero not only survives but thrives, beginning to glimpse the eternal truths that lie beyond the illusion of separation.

Throughout this Journey, the Hero is guided by mentors, allies, and divine forces. These guides may take many forms an elder, a spiritual teacher, a sacred text, or a synchronistic encounter. These guides offer guidance and sacred tools maps or mantras, meditations, and rituals that equip the Hero for the trials ahead. Yet it becomes clear along the quest that the true guide on this Journey is the Hero's higher self, the voice of the soul that whispers the truth in moments of silence and stillness.

At the heart of the Hero's Journey lies the abyss a metaphorical place of profound darkness and despair, where the Hero must confront their deepest fears. This is the point of greatest vulnerability, where the Hero feels utterly alone, disconnected from all they once knew. It is also the point of greatest potential, where the Hero must relinquish their ego, surrender completely to the divine will and allow the unfolding of the cosmic plan. It is a moment of profound transformation, where the Hero's old self dies, and a new, enlightened version of themselves is born.

This moment of surrender marks the Hero's death and rebirth. The Hero touches the divine, experiencing a moment of profound enlightenment, where the illusion of separation is dissolved, and the Hero realises their unity with the cosmos. They emerge from this abyss transformed, carrying within them the sacred truth they have sought, an elixir that has the power to heal, enlighten, and bring about profound change.

The challenge is not completed until the Hero has reached home with this experience. The return home is the final stage of the Hero's Journey, but it is not a return to the life they once knew. The Hero has been irrevocably changed, and so too has their world.

They bring with them the gifts of their Journey, the wisdom, the courage, and the love that they have cultivated. These gifts are not for the Hero alone but for the community, the world, and the cosmos. In sharing them, the Hero fulfils their true purpose, becoming a living embodiment of the divine and strengthening the bonds of our shared humanity.

The moment of transformation in the Shero's Journey is a sacred union a merging of the self with the divine, of the inner and the outer, the blending of light and the dark. In this sacred union, the Shero experiences a profound sense of wholeness, of being at one with the universe. She realises that her Journey is not separate from the Journey of the earth, the moon, or the stars but is part of the great cosmic dance.

As she returns from this Journey, the Shero carries with her the sacred gifts of the feminine intuition, compassion, creativity, and the power to nurture and heal. She brings these gifts into the world not to conquer but to create, not to dominate but to sustain. The Shero's Journey is one of service, of giving back to the earth, the community, and the future.

THE SHERO'S JOURNEY: THE SACRED DANCE OF LIFE

For centuries, the Hero's Journey has dominated the narratives of transformation, celebrating outward quests and the conquest of challenges. Yet, woven alongside this archetype is another path, one just as profound, though often overlooked: the Shero's Journey. This sacred path honours the rhythms of nature, the wisdom of the body, and the deep, transformative power of healing. It calls us inward, to the sacred centre of ourselves, to navigate the cycles of life, death, and rebirth.

Unlike the linear path of the Hero, the Shero's Journey is cyclical, mirroring the phases of the moon and the seasons of the earth. It invites us to listen, feel, and embrace the full spectrum of our emotions not to conquer, but to commune. The Shero's Journey is one of integration, weaving together the light and shadow of life into a tapestry of wholeness.

ANSWERING THE CALL OF THE SHERO

I first heard the call of the Shero's Journey during a time of deep introspection. After years of twice daily meditation, my inner landscape had become familiar, a sanctuary where I could meet myself fully. By the end of 2011, I felt drawn to deepen my meditation practice further. This pull led me to Rishikesh, India a place where the ancient wisdom of the divine feminine felt palpable in the air.

I lived at an ashram, rising before dawn each day for sadhana. The dark December mornings were cold and still, the only sound the distant murmur of the River Ganges. In this sacred silence, I encountered not only the goddess within but also the shadows I had long avoided. Guided by the rhythms of this sacred land, I began to embrace the cyclical nature of the Shero's Journey.

The river Ganga herself seemed to echo this truth, her waters flowing endlessly in a cycle of renewal and release. As I stood on her banks, I realised that this journey was not about grand gestures or external accomplishments. It was about honouring the quiet whispers of intuition, trusting the flow of life, and allowing the divine feminine to guide me home to myself.

TOOLS FOR THE SHERO'S JOURNEY

The Shero does not walk this path empty-handed. Guided by the wisdom of the sacred feminine, she carries tools that nurture, protect, and empower her. These tools are not swords or shields but herbs, crystals, rituals, and prayers that weave a web of life.

- **Herbs and Plants:** Mugwort for dreamwork, Rose petals for self- love, lavender for calm each herb carries a frequency that supports the Shero's healing.
- **Crystals:** Moonstone for intuition, amethyst for clarity, rose quartz for the heart these stones amplify the Shero's connection to her inner wisdom.
- **Rituals:** Lighting a candle to honour her journey, journaling under the full moon to release and call in or creating an altar as a sacred touchstone.
- **Prayers:** Simple, heartfelt words spoken aloud or silently, weaving the Shero's intention into the fabric of the universe.

The Transformation of the Shero

The moment of transformation in the Shero's Journey is not a triumphant victory but a sacred union a merging of the self with the divine, the inner and the outer, the light and the dark. In this sacred union, the Shero experiences a profound sense of wholeness, realising that she is not separate from the cycles of life, but she is an integral part of the great cosmic dance. In this way, she becomes the guardian of life, the keeper of the sacred flame.

The Sacred Integration: Walking the Path of Wholeness

As we honour the Shero's Journey, we begin to see that her path is an essential counterpart of the Hero's Quest. Together, they form the tapestry of our spiritual awakening. In truth, the Hero's Journey and the Shero's Journey are not separate paths but two halves of a sacred whole. Each of us carries within us both the Hero and the Shero, the sacred masculine and the sacred feminine. To walk the path of wholeness is to honour and integrate both energies within our being.

Just as the sun and moon share the sky, the Hero and Shero illuminate different aspects of our soul's journey. The Hero teaches us to seek, strive, and conquer our inner demons. The Shero teaches us to listen, feel, and heal our inner wounds. Together, they guide us towards a state of balance, where we are strong and compassionate, courageous and nurturing, wise and loving.

HONOURING YOUR INNER HERO AND SHERO

As you walk your own path, notice and remember all the ways that you are both the Hero and the Shero. Honour your soul's call, trust in your heart's wisdom, and know that every step you take is a sacred act of creation. Embrace the trials and the triumphs, the light and the dark, the joy and the sorrow, for they are all part of the sacred journey of your soul.

By walking these paths, we not only transform ourselves but contribute to the healing and awakening of the world. In embracing both the Hero and the Shero, we become the guardians of a new harmony one that honours the sacred in all things.

THE TRIALS OF THE SHERO

The trials on the Shero's Journey are not external battles but inner reckonings. They are the heart's wounds, the soul's shadows, and the buried truths that must be unearthed and embraced. These trials demand vulnerability, courage, and compassion not to overcome them but to integrate. Through this process, the Shero discovers that her wounds are not weaknesses but doorways to her greatest strength.

Grief may arise as a teacher, asking us to sit with its weight and honour its wisdom. Fear may emerge as a mirror, reflecting the parts of ourselves we have yet to love. These experiences are not obstacles but invitations to heal not just for us but for our ancestors and future generations.

Reflective Prompts for the Shero's Path

To walk the Shero's Journey is to honour the sacred feminine within. Consider these prompts as you reflect on your own path:

- What emotions or truths are calling for your attention and integration?
- How can you create space for stillness and listening in your daily life?
- What rituals or tools help you connect with the sacred feminine?
- In what ways can you offer the gifts of your healing journey to the world?

Sacred Rituals for Integration

Daily rituals are the key to this sacred integration. Through meditation, prayer, journaling, and communion with nature, we can attune to both the Hero and the Shero within us. These rituals allow us to tap into the power of the sacred masculine when we need strength and courage and to draw on the wisdom of the sacred feminine when we need guidance and healing.

REFLECTION

Take a moment to reflect:

What daily practices can you cultivate to balance the Hero and Shero within you? Consider journaling on how these energies show up in your life and where they may need greater harmony.

BECOMING THE GUARDIANS OF THE SACRED FLAME

In the end, the Hero's Journey and the Shero's Journey are not just stories; they are the living, breathing truth of our existence. They are the sacred paths that lead us home to ourselves, to find each other, and to the divine.

By consciously cultivating both energies in our daily lives, we create a sacred space within us where the Hero and the Shero can meet, merge, and dance. This dance is the dance of life, the dance of the cosmos, the dance of the divine. It is the path of wholeness, the path of spiritual awakening, and the path of true enlightenment.

Through the integration of these energies, we become not just the heroes and sheroes of our own lives but also the creators of our collective destiny.

By nurturing this balance within, we ignite the sacred flame of life a flame that illuminates our path, strengthens our connections, and inspires us to walk in harmony with the universe.

This is not mythology. This is your life. By honouring the Hero and the Shero within, you become a living temple, where action and presence, seeking and surrender, dance as one.

You become the guardian of your sacred flame.
A carrier of light.
A teacher through being.

As your journey deepens, the world is changed quietly, undeniably, by your presence.

Because you didn't just walk the path.
You became it.

Chapter 20
Embracing Shadow:
Sacred Journey of Inner Growth

Descent Into the Self

The fire crackled softly in the dimly lit room, shadows flickering against the walls. A group of us sat in quiet reflection, the air thick with an unspoken anticipation. That evening, we had gathered for deep shadow work a journey inward to meet the hidden parts of ourselves.

As the silence stretched, I became aware of a stirring deep within me, a restlessness I could not quite name. A slow unease crept into my body, a tightening in my chest, an ache in my belly.

My breath grew shallow, as if something long buried was rising from the depths, seeking to be seen. My teacher's voice broke the silence. "Close your eyes. Breathe. What are you afraid to see?"

A rush of memories flooded my mind old wounds, long-forgotten fears, echoes of words that had once cut deeply. I felt the weight of them pressing in, not as an enemy, but as a long-lost part of myself waiting to be acknowledged. The discomfort intensified, sharp and insistent, demanding my presence. For a moment, I wanted to turn away, to escape back into the safety of the known. But instead, I stayed. I listened.

And then, something shifted. The tightness in my chest softened, the weight of unspoken fears began to unravel. Awareness seeped in, slow and steady, like the first light of dawn breaking through the darkness. In that moment, I understood shadow work is not about eliminating darkness, but about making space for all that we are, standing in the fullness of our truth.

The Path of Wholeness

In the quest for spiritual awakening, we often seek the warmth and clarity of the light the aspects of ourselves that exude love, joy, and wisdom. Yet, true wholeness embraces both light and darkness, the seen and the unseen, the acknowledged and the hidden.

Shadow work is the sacred practice of exploring and accepting the concealed parts of ourselves the fears, wounds, and desires that reside in the depths of our subconscious. It is an act of courage, a journey that leads to deeper authenticity, compassion, and connection with the divine.

Understanding the Shadow: The Hidden Self

The shadow embodies the facets of ourselves that we have repressed, denied, or overlooked throughout our lives. These may include unresolved traumas, suppressed emotions, unmet needs, and even latent talents and aspirations.

Often, these aspects have been buried due to societal expectations, cultural conditioning, or personal experiences that taught us which parts of ourselves were acceptable and which were not.

We suppress anger to be seen as kind. We hide vulnerability to appear strong. We diminish our gifts for fear of standing out. Yet, when these hidden aspects remain unacknowledged, they manifest as self-sabotage, limiting beliefs, and unconscious patterns that hold us back. Shadow work is a radical act of self-love. It asks us to meet these hidden parts with compassion rather than fear, to listen instead of reject. As we do, we uncover the wisdom that was buried beneath our wounds, transforming our fears into strength and our pain into understanding.

THE SACRED NATURE OF SHADOW WORK

Shadow work is sacred because it requires deep honesty and reverence for the whole self. Mystics such as Rumi have spoken of the shadow as a path to inner wholeness. His poetry reminds us that what we resist often holds the greatest wisdom, and that by embracing our full spectrum of emotions, we step closer to the divine.

> *"The wound is the place where the light enters you."* Rumi

Engaging in shadow work is an alchemical process one that transmutes pain into wisdom, fear into love, and fragmentation into wholeness. As we acknowledge our shadows, we no longer project them onto others. Instead, we reclaim ourselves, leading to deeper relationships, greater self- awareness, and a profound connection to the divine.

THE SHADOW AS A SACRED QUADRANT

In the sacred geometry of the Mandala of Wisdom, each aspect of our being is represented as an interconnected pattern light and shadow in perfect harmony. One quadrant is dimly lit, holding the unspoken fears, hidden wounds, and untapped potential of your shadow. With each breath, imagine this space glowing softly, merging with the whole. In this integration, you are not erasing the shadow, but welcoming it home.

As you delve into the shadow, you might visualise the mandala, allowing its structure to guide you through the process. Within this mandala, the shadow is not an obstacle but a necessary part of wholeness. Just as the light and shadow of night and day coexist, so too must we embrace the totality of our being.

The Mandala as a Guide for Shadow Work

When engaging in shadow work, the mandala can help you navigate through the complexities of the subconscious. Each symbol and pattern within the mandala can represent different aspects of the shadow fears, desires, wounds, or hidden talents. You can personalise your mandala by assigning specific symbols to recurring themes in your shadow. For example, you might choose a spiral to represent recurring patterns, a tree for growth emerging from past wounds, or a flame to symbolise transformation of fear into courage. By meditating on these symbols, you can bring clarity to the areas of your shadow that need attention and integration.

Integrating Shadow Work into the Mandala of Wisdom

- **The Spiral:** As you confront recurring patterns or unresolved issues in your life, the spiral can symbolise your journey towards higher understanding. Reflect on how you are revisiting old wounds with greater awareness, spiralling upwards in your spiritual evolution.
- **The Lotus:** As you work through difficult emotions or

memories, the lotus can remind you of the potential for transformation and rebirth. Just as the lotus rises from the mud to bloom in purity, your shadow work can emerge from the mud of experiences and lead to spiritual enlightenment and growth.

Completing the Mandala: The Role of Shadow Integration

Completing the mandala of your inner wisdom requires the integration of all its parts, including the shadow. The mandala becomes a living, evolving symbol as you integrate insights and experiences gained through shadow work.

With each new layer of understanding, the mandala transforms, reflecting the dynamic interplay between light and shadow within you. Visualise this process as a continuous unfolding a sacred dance where each piece of wisdom you uncover weaves a new thread into the intricate tapestry of your inner world.

The Mandala of Wisdom is an active process, not just a passive symbol; it is an evolving representation of your journey towards spiritual wholeness. By engaging with your shadow through the lens of the mandala, you can see more clearly how each piece of your inner world fits together, leading towards a more balanced and enlightened existence.

The Process of Shadow Work: A Journey Inward

As you work through your shadow, you are essentially filling in the missing pieces of the mandala, bringing it closer to completion.

Each time you embrace a part of your shadow, you add to the mandala's vibrancy and depth, making it a true reflection of your whole self. Embarking on the journey of shadow work involves several steps, each requiring patience, honesty, and self-compassion as you engage more deeply with your shadow.

Cultivating Self-Awareness

The first step in shadow work is developing a heightened sense of self awareness. This involves observing your thoughts, emotions, and behaviours without judgement. Pay attention to intense emotional reactions and situations that trigger discomfort or defensiveness. These responses often signal the presence of shadow aspects seeking acknowledgment and integration.

Creating a Safe and Sacred Space

Shadow work requires a supportive environment where you feel safe to explore and express vulnerable emotions. Create a physical and psychological space that offers comfort and tranquility. This could be a quiet room with items that hold spiritual significance for you. Establishing a ritual, lighting a candle or saying a prayer before your practice, can help set a sacred tone and intention for your journey inward.

Reflective Practices and Techniques

Various practices can facilitate deep exploration and integration of the shadow:

- **Journaling:** Writing allows you to process and articulate complex emotions and thoughts. Prompt yourself with questions like, "What situations make me feel uncomfortable?" and reflect on why? or "What qualities do I dislike in others?" and reflect on the possibility that they might reflect aspects of myself?
- **Meditation:** Mindful meditation helps you observe your inner world with clarity and compassion. Guided meditations focusing on shadow integration can assist in connecting with suppressed emotions and memories.
- **Dream Analysis:** Dreams often reveal hidden aspects of the subconscious. Keeping a dream journal and reflecting on recurring themes or symbols can provide insights into your shadow.
- **Creative Expression:** Art, music, and movement offer powerful avenues to explore and express shadow elements non-verbally. Engaging in creative activities can unlock emotions and perspectives that are difficult to access through logical analysis alone.

Therapeutic Support: Working with a therapist, counsellor, or spiritual mentor can provide guidance, support, and objective perspectives as you navigate the complexities of shadow work.

PRACTISING COMPASSION AND ACCEPTANCE

As you uncover shadow aspects of yourself, the process of releasing and transforming is not about blaming others or shaming yourself. Offer forgiveness to yourself and others who were involved in past wounds, understanding that healing is about integrating the shadow sides. Recognise that these parts of yourself have formed as responses to past experiences and have served a purpose in your survival and development. Approach them with unconditional love and acceptance.

INTEGRATING AND HEALING

Integration involves consciously incorporating insights and lessons gained from shadow work into your daily life. This may show up as shifting perspectives, adopting new behaviours, and making empowered choices that reflect your authentic self. Celebrate your progress and acknowledge the courage it takes to engage in this deep work. Remember that integration is an ongoing process and be patient with yourself as you continue to evolve.

THE DANGER OF SPIRITUAL BYPASSING: AVOIDING THE SHADOW

It is tempting to focus only on the light, avoiding pain or uncomfortable truths. This is known as spiritual bypassing using spiritual practices to suppress deeper healing. True enlightenment is not found in escaping discomfort, but in learning to hold both joy and sorrow, expansion and contraction, love and loss, with grace.

Spiritual bypassing can create a superficial sense of well-being, masking underlying pain and preventing true healing and growth. It perpetuates disconnection from the authentic self and can lead to judgement, denial, and a lack of empathy towards oneself and others.

Acknowledging and embracing the shadow is essential to prevent spiritual bypassing. It grounds our spiritual practice and authenticity, allowing us to experience the full spectrum of human emotion and experience. By facing our shadows, we develop resilience, depth, and a more profound capacity for love and compassion. This holistic approach to spirituality honours the complexity of our existence and cultivates genuine transformation and enlightenment.

The Gifts of Shadow Work: Transformation and Growth

The journey through the shadow yields profound gifts and insights that enrich every aspect of our lives:

Enhanced Self-Awareness and Authenticity

Shadow work unveils the truths hidden within us, enabling us to live more authentically and align our actions with our deepest values and desires. We become more honest with ourselves and others, developing genuine connections and fulfilling relationships.

Emotional Healing and Resilience

By confronting and healing past wounds, we release emotional burdens and patterns that have held us back. This process builds emotional resilience, empowering us to navigate life's challenges with grace and equanimity.

Increased Empathy and Compassion

Understanding and integrating our own shadows cultivates empathy and compassion for the struggles and imperfections of others. We recognise the shared humanity in our collective experiences, which enables more harmonious interactions.

Unlocking Creative and Spiritual Potential

Reclaiming suppressed aspects of ourselves liberates creative and spiritual energy that can be channeled into personal expression, innovation, and deeper spiritual practices. We tap into a wellspring of inspiration and insight that enhances our contributions to the world.

INNER PEACE AND WHOLENESS

Integration of the shadow brings a profound sense of inner peace and completeness. When we reconcile conflicting aspects within ourselves, we reduce the inner turmoil which leads to a more balanced state of being.

EMBRACING THE SHADOW AS A LIFELONG PRACTICE

Shadow work is not a one-time session; it is a lifelong commitment to self- discovery and evolution. As we journey through different phases of life, new layers of the shadow may surface, inviting us to delve deeper into our inner landscape.

- **Regular Self-Reflection:** Incorporate moments of introspection into your daily or weekly routine to stay attuned to your inner state.
- **Stay Open and Curious:** Approach new insights and challenges with an open mind and a willingness to learn and grow.
- **Seek Support and Community:** Engage with supportive individuals and communities that strengthen understanding and encourage personal growth.
- **Practise Self-Care:** Prioritise activities and habits that nurture your physical, emotional, and spiritual well-being.
- **Celebrate Your Growth:** Acknowledge and honour the progress you make along your journey, no matter how small.

- **Reflective Exercises for Engaging with Your Shadow:** To deepen your engagement with shadow work, you could try the following exercises:
- **Mirror Dialogue:** Stand before a mirror and look into your own eyes. Speak openly about your fears, regrets, and desires. Allow whatever emotions arise to surface without judgement. Affirm love and acceptance for yourself, acknowledging your light and shadow.
- **Track Your Triggers:** Notice moments when you feel strong emotional reactions. Record these instances in a journal, making a note of the situation, and explore your feelings and any thoughts that arise. Reflect on possible underlying causes or past experiences that remind you of similar feelings that may be connected to these reactions.
- **Inner Child Meditation:** Sit comfortably and close your eyes, taking deep, calming breaths. Visualise yourself as a child in a safe and peaceful setting. Engage in a conversation with this younger self, offering comfort, understanding, and unconditional love. Listen to any messages or needs expressed by your inner child and affirm your commitment to nurturing and protecting them.
- **Creative Expression:** Choose a form of creative expression that resonates with you drawing, writing, dancing, painting. Use this to explore and portray aspects of your shadow. Allow yourself to express the feeling freely without worrying how the finished painting looks. Reflect on the emotions and insights that emerge through this process.

EMBRACING WHOLENESS THROUGH SHADOW WORK

The journey of shadow work is a profound act of self-love and spiritual devotion. By courageously exploring and integrating the hidden aspects of ourselves, we step into our true power and authenticity. We come to understand that our shadows are not burdens to be carried; they are inner treasures to be discovered, offering invaluable lessons and opportunities for transformation. May the light and shadow within you dance together in harmony, creating the masterpiece of your soul.

As you embark on this sacred journey, may you be guided by compassion, courage, and unwavering love for yourself. Embrace the shadows with the same reverence as the light, knowing that both are essential facets of your divine essence. Through this integration, may you find deeper connection, purpose, and joy, illuminating your path and inspiring others to embark on their own journeys of self-discovery and healing.

By weaving shadow work into the Mandala of Wisdom, you create a living, dynamic representation of your spiritual journey one that honours the complexity and beauty of your entire being. As you continue to explore and integrate the various aspects of yourself both light and shadow you bring the Mandala of Wisdom to life, creating a harmonious and complete tapestry of your soul's journey.

Shadow work is not a single moment it is an ongoing relationship with the self. Each time we sit with our darkness rather than running from it, we strengthen our capacity for love, wisdom, and presence. Regular reflection, openness, and community support help us navigate this sacred work. By weaving shadow work into the Mandala of Wisdom, we create a living, dynamic representation of our spiritual journey one that honours the complexity and beauty of our entire being.

Shadow work is not a one time session; it is a lifelong commitment to self- discovery and evolution. As we journey through different phases of life, new layers of the shadow may surface, inviting us to delve deeper into our inner landscape. May you walk this path with courage, knowing that your shadows do not diminish you. They are the gateways to your greatest transformation.

You Are Already Whole

The Mandala of Wisdom is not a symbol.
It is your life.
Your breath.
Your becoming...

Each time you enter the dark with courage,
Each time you love what once scared you,
Each time you soften when you could judge

You complete another piece of the pattern.
You don't need to fear the shadow.
It's not your enemy.
It's your invitation.

And when you embrace it, you remember:
You were never broken.
You were always whole.

Chapter 21
The Wheel of the Year: Sabbats and Solstices

The Call of Avalon

For months, Avalon had been pulling me towards her mysteries. I dreamt of bathing in sacred springs, of walking through mist-laden hills, of entering places where time folded in on itself. So, on the cusp of my birthday, I took Luna with me for a few days of quiet pilgrimage, staying at the foot of the Tor, where the White and Red Springs flow twin rivers of alchemy, one clear, one tinged with the lifeblood of the earth.

I knew this was a threshold. It was not just a journey to Glastonbury, but a crossing that would change me. I was deep into my shamanic path, and the call of the ancient land was growing louder, more insistent.

It whispered in the winds, wound itself through my dreams, and echoed in the symbols that kept appearing labyrinths, spirals, serpents coiling through time.

That evening, I stepped into the White Spring.

The air was thick with incense, floral and soft, like midnight jasmine floating through the dark. The steady trickle of water echoed through the cavern, a song older than memory. Candles flickered against the stone walls, their light casting shifting shadows, as if unseen figures danced in the periphery. I removed my shoes and stepped barefoot onto the cool, wet ground, feeling the pulse of something ancient beneath me.

This was not just a sacred site. It was a portal. A liminal space. A remembering. Kneeling by the water, I dipped my hands into its cool, flowing embrace. The moment my skin touched the surface, something stirred. A current of energy rippled through me not just water, but memory, an imprint of something I had always known but had somehow forgotten.

That night, as I lay beneath the watchful presence of the Tor, I dreamt of the labyrinth again. I saw the spirals, the winding path, the serpents coiling through the unseen realms. And when I woke, I understood Avalon is never just a place. It is a state of being, a rhythm, a cycle that calls to those who are ready.

As we tune into the wheel of the year, we surrender to the ancient rhythms that Avalon, the Tor, and the sacred waters have always sung. To live in harmony with the Wheel is to live in harmony with the great mysteries themselves.

WALKING THE SPIRAL, REMEMBERING THE WAY

To walk the Wheel of the Year is to walk an ancient spiral the rhythm of the land, the breath of the cosmos, the pulse of the soul. It is not a belief system, but a remembering. A way of being in relationship with the changing seasons, the shifts of light and dark, and the natural cycles that guide all of life.

These rhythms are part of the ancient lands, once woven into the very fabric of village life. Before calendars and clocks, there was the sun and the land the first green shoots, the ripening grain, the returning dark.

These festivals of the turning of the year were sacred moments in time to gather to celebrate, to dance, to feast, to make offerings. Each festival marked the turning points of the year of planting and gathering in the harvest and of celebrating the community's connection to the earth and nature.

The Wheel of the Year is the breath of the earth, the great turning, the cosmic spiral that guides us through the ever-changing dance of life, death, and rebirth, in a living mandala of transformation, and rebirth and renewal. To live in harmony with the Wheel is to live in harmony with the great mysteries themselves.

For me, the Wheel is not only a calendar, but a mandala a sacred pattern that mirrors the cycles of transformation I have witnessed within myself and those I teach in our spirals. The wheel of the year turning teaches me that nothing is static, that everything from the new bud of spring to the stillness of midwinter has its rightful place in the spiral of becoming.

It was Avalon that first opened this portal. The land itself Glastonbury, the Tor, the sacred springs whispered a language older than words, a rhythm I felt in my bones. I came to see that the Wheel was not only turning around me... it was turning through me.

This chapter is a guide to remembering that rhythm of the year as a framework to hold your own seasons of growth, rest, power, and renewal. A way to live in tune with the pulse of the earth, elements, nature and community.

THE WHEEL OF THE YEAR: A SACRED FRAMEWORK

The Wheel of the Year is more than a calendar it is a living rhythm, a way of aligning our own cycles with the rhythms of nature. It is a sacred map woven into the fabric of time, guiding us through the eternal dance of light and dark, growth and rest, life and renewal. Rooted in Celtic, Norse, and pre-Christian agricultural traditions, this cycle of eight festivals the Greater Sabbats and Lesser Sabbats honours the shifting energies of the Earth and the cosmos. Each season brings its own initiation a call to turn inward or to step forward, to plant or to harvest, to release or to receive.

Samhain invites us to walk the liminal spaces, honouring our ancestors and embracing the unseen. Beltane urges us to ignite our passions, to create, to dance in the firelight of possibility. Yule reminds us that even in darkness, the light is reborn, while Litha teaches us to celebrate life at its peak.

By aligning with these ancient festivals, we do more than observe the changing seasons we step into their wisdom, allowing their rhythms to shape and inspire our spiritual journey. Each turn of the Wheel invites reflection, celebration, and transformation, offering a chance to synchronise with nature's pulse and deepen our connection to the land, the elements, and ourselves.

Each festival represents a petal of this great mandala, a place to pause, reflect, and realign. Just as the seasons change, so do we. By stepping into the rhythm of the Wheel, we align with the wisdom of the land, the cycles of the cosmos, and the deep, ancient knowing that we, too, are part of this great dance.

The Wheel of the Year is more than a calendar of seasonal celebrations; it is a way of aligning our own cycles with the rhythms of nature. Each season brings its own initiation a call to turn inward or to step forward, to plant or to harvest, to release or to receive.

The Eight Sabbats: Gateways Through the Year

The Greater Sabbats mark the powerful cross-quarter days, the liminal midpoints between solstices and equinoxes. These festivals carry heightened energy, moments of potent transformation.

The Lesser Sabbats align with the solstices and equinoxes, celebrating the balance and shifting tides of light and dark. Each festival is a threshold, a doorway into deeper awareness and connection.

Greater Sabbats (Cross-Quarter Days)

Imbolc (1–2 February) The First Stirring of Light
Imbolc marks the quickening of life beneath the frost, the first whisper of spring. It is a time of purification, renewal, and planting seeds of intention, both literal and spiritual.

Themes: New beginnings, inner cleansing, inspiration.
Traditions: Lighting candles, honouring Brigid, setting intentions for the year ahead.

Beltane (30 April–1 May) – The Fire of Passion and Fertility
Beltane is wild, untamed, alive with fire and desire. The land is abundant, fertile, bursting into bloom. It is a time to celebrate creativity, love, and vitality, to step fully into our power.

Themes: Fertility, passion, creative energy, divine union.
Traditions: Bonfires, maypole dancing, handfasting ceremonies.

Lughnasadh (1–2 August) – The First Harvest
Lughnasadh (Loo-nass-ah) is the festival of the first fruits, the sacred moment of reaping what has been sown. It reminds us to give thanks, share abundance, and recognise the effort behind our achievements.

Themes: Gratitude, abundance, personal and communal success.
Traditions: Feasting, baking bread, honouring the land's gifts.

Samhain (31 October–1 November) – The Veil is Thin
Samhain is the gateway between worlds, the festival where the past and present touch, where the ancestors walk beside us. It is a time of deep reflection, endings, and transformation.

Themes: Death and rebirth, ancestral connection, shadow work
Traditions: Honouring the dead, lighting lanterns, divination

LESSER SABBATS (QUARTER DAYS)

Yule (Winter Solstice, 20–23 December) – The Rebirth of Light
The longest night of the year holds the promise of renewal. Yule reminds us that even in darkness, the light is being reborn. It is a festival of hope, warmth, and rekindling the inner flame.

Themes: Renewal, inner light, cycles of death and rebirth
Traditions: Decorating evergreens, lighting candles, gift-giving

Ostara (Spring Equinox, 19–23 March) – Balance and Awakening
At Ostara, day and night stand equal before the sun's growing strength tips the balance towards light and expansion. It is a time

of fertility, fresh starts, and honouring the earth's awakening.

Themes: Renewal, balance, planting new intentions
Traditions: Egg symbolism, nature walks, seed planting

Litha (Summer Solstice, 19–23 June) – The Sun at its Zenith

The longest day of the year, Litha is a celebration of power, joy, and boundless life force. It invites us to stand fully in our light and embrace our vitality.

Themes: Power, abundance, divine energy
Traditions: Bonfires, sun rituals, connecting with nature's peak energy

Mabon (Autumn Equinox, 19–23 September) – The Balance of Light and Dark

Mabon is the turning towards stillness, the moment of balance before the descent into winter. It is a time for gratitude, reflection, and preparing for the inward journey ahead.

Themes: Harvest, gratitude, equilibrium
Traditions: Feasting, honouring the land, autumn rituals

LIVING IN RHYTHM WITH THE WHEEL OF THE YEAR

Meditation and Reflection: Aligning the Inner and Outer Cycles

Each festival invites us to pause and listen to the land, to ourselves, to the wisdom of the turning year.

- **Imbolc:** What new light is stirring within me?
- **Beltane:** Where is my passion guiding me?
- **Lughnasadh:** What am I harvesting in my life?
- **Samhain:** What do I need to release?

- **Yule:** How can I embrace stillness and renewal?
- **Ostara:** What is beginning to awaken within me?
- **Litha:** How can I stand in my full power?
- **Mabon:** Where in my life do I need balance?

Rituals and Sacred Practices

Honouring the Wheel of the Year can be as simple or as ceremonial as you feel called too.

- **Imbolc** – Light a white candle and set an intention for renewal.
- **Beltane** – Dance, create, embrace the joy of the season.
- **Lughnasadh** – Bake bread, share a meal in gratitude.
- **Samhain** – Light a candle for an ancestor, journal on personal transformation.
- **Yule** – Reflect by candlelight, celebrate small joys.
- **Ostara** – Plant seeds, walk in nature, create something new.
- **Litha** – Meditate in the sun, celebrate your vitality.
- **Mabon** – Reflect on the year so far, express gratitude.

A BLESSING FOR EACH TURN OF THE YEAR

Imbolc – The First Light
"May I honour the first stirrings of light within me. May I tend the flame of inspiration, and trust what is beginning to rise."
What seed am I planting in my life right now?

Ostara – The Spring Balance
"May I walk in balance as light and dark meet as equals. May I awaken with the Earth and greet this new beginning with grace."

What is seeking to grow through me?

Beltane – The Fire of Becoming
"May I celebrate the passion of life and the joy of creation. May I dance with the fire of possibility and open to divine union."

Where am I being called to ignite my creative power?

Litha – The Height of the Sun
"May I stand fully in my light. May I radiate with vitality, gratitude, and abundance."

How can I honour the peak of my power with humility and joy?

Lughnasadh – The First Harvest
"May I give thanks for the fruits of my labour. May I honour the cycles of effort, gratitude, and release."

What am I harvesting in my life at this time?

Mabon – The Sacred Balance
"May I find harmony in all things — within and without. May I pause and reflect before the descent into the quiet season."

What am I being invited to let go of to restore balance?

Samhain – The Veil is Thin
"May I honour those who came before me and listen for their wisdom. May I walk the shadowed path with courage and compassion."

What is ready to be laid to rest? What wants to be transformed?

Yule – The Rebirth of Light

"May I find peace in the stillness. May I trust in the returning light, both around me and within me."

What light is quietly being reborn within me during this time of darkness?

SEASONAL SHIFTS

Reflection: Your Journey Through the Wheel

The Wheel of the Year is not an external cycle of dates and seasons it is a rhythm that runs through the land, the body, and the soul. It is an ancient inheritance, passed down through the soil and the stars, asking only that we remember.

It is a sacred mandala of transformation, a mirror of our own inner landscapes. We return to the rhythm of nature, of the ancestors. We realign with the path of deep knowing, when to take sacred pause, and when to plant new action, and when to celebrate the results with joyful embodiment.

Ask yourself:
- What is blossoming within me this spring?
- What am I ready to shed as the leaves fall?
- Where is the light returning in my life?
- What does my soul want to harvest?

This is your invitation to step into the dance to walk the spiral not as an observer, but as a participant. To light the candles, bless the seeds, share the feast, sing into the night. To let the sacred live through you, season by season. Because to live in harmony with the Wheel is to remember: *You are nature. You are rhythm. You are sacred.*

THE SPIRAL PATH HOME

To live in rhythm with the Wheel of the Year is to walk the spiral path of remembrance. It is to let the earth teach us how to soften, how to rise, how to root, and how to release. These ancient gateways—Imbolc's first light, Beltane's fire, Samhain's shadow—are not only thresholds in time; they are initiations of the soul.

CHAPTER 22
MOON CYCLES:
REFLECTION AND MANIFESTATION

On a New Moon, our circle began a series of lunar ceremonies, honouring the ancient land, in the sacred space of stillness in my little garden haven. The yurt in my garden was a place of deep initiation into the mysteries and became the portal for my transmissions. I would sit, listening to the wind weaving through the tall trees, resting in the hum of nature, receiving its silent wisdom.

For much of my life, the moon has been my companion, her phases mirroring the rhythms within my own body. For most of my menstruating bleeding years, I felt her presence deeply her cycle intertwined with my own. Now, in the shifting landscape of perimenopause and menopause, I see Grandmother Moon differently. She is no longer just a reflection of my inner tides but a beacon in the sky, illuminating my path through this transition.

I watch the moon rise through my kitchen window, her silver light shimmering through the branches of the ancient trees. Later, as I draw the curtains, she remains present waxing, waning, or glowing in her fullness an unwavering presence that whispers, "You are still part of this cycle. You are still held in the embrace of time."

This is the wisdom of the moon that no phase is ever lost, only transformed. Just as she disappears into darkness only to be reborn, so too do we navigate our own cycles of renewal, release, and rebirth. This cyclical movement is a testament to the interconnectedness of all life, serving not only as a celestial phenomenon but also as a guide, a cosmic compass that points us toward a deeper understanding of our inner and outer worlds.

For some, this connection is reflected in their monthly cycle, while for others, it manifests through emotional tides, creative surges, or moments of stillness and renewal. No matter how we experience it, the moon remains a constant guide, holding space for our journey.

A Poem to Her Rhythm

In the quiet darkness, the New Moon whispers, Seeds of dreams in shadows are planted. Crescent light, a tender bloom of hope, Promise and potential softly emerge. Halfway shines the Quarter's face, Challenges met with unwavering grace. Gibbous swells, nearing full embrace, Intentions ripen, taking their place. Full Moon bright, in silver glow, revealing all that we must know. Release the old, let burdens fall, in her light, the truth stands tall. Waning now, the moon's retreat, Lessons learned, reflections sweet. Crescent fades, a gentle swoon, Rest and dream beneath the moon.

The Sacred Feminine in Lunar Cycles

The moon is a compass of the divine feminine reflecting our emotions, creativity, and inner knowing. Regardless of gender, we all hold this interplay of sacred feminine (receptivity, flow) and sacred masculine (structure, action). By aligning with lunar rhythms, we honour both energies and activate a cycle of conscious co-creation. Each moon phase holds unique energy for growth, reflection, and transformation. With 13 lunar cycles each year, the moon offers us rhythmic invitations for pause, presence, and purposeful action. For those who menstruate, the alignment with the cycle deepens body-wisdom. For those beyond, the moon becomes a mirror of evolution and archetypal wisdom.

LUNAR PHASES

The moon's phases offer universal energies that everyone can harness for personal growth and transformation. Each phase of the moon carries a unique vibration expanding, peaking, waning, and releasing mirroring the rhythms of life itself. By consciously attuning to these cycles, we cultivate a practice of deep listening: to the universe, to our bodies, and to the quiet wisdom that speaks in stillness.

Each moon phase has its unique energy and symbolism, echoing the natural flow of life. By understanding and working with these phases, we can tap into the moon's influence to enhance our rituals, heal our wounds, and align our intentions with the universe's greater plan. These lunar cycles offer a rhythmic cadence to our lives, much like a heartbeat pulsing through time reminding us to pause, reflect, and honour the sacred transitions within.

Just as it takes 365 days for the Earth to orbit the sun, the moon completes its orbit around the Earth in approximately 28 days, resulting in 13 moon cycles annually. These lunar cycles offer a rhythmic cadence to our lives, providing natural checkpoints for reflection, intention-setting, and release. For women, the menstrual cycle can serve as an alignment, where the moon and menstruation phases work together to deepen our connection to our bodies, emotions, and spiritual growth.

Moon Cycle for Self-Reflection

The moon's phases have been revered throughout history for their profound influence on various aspects of life, from agriculture to spiritual practices. Each lunar phase brings a different energy, which can be harnessed for specific healing processes, rituals, and self-reflection.

Rituals for the Waxing Crescent

- **Goal Planning:** Create actionable steps towards your goals and dreams. Visualise your intentions growing and expanding.
- **Creative Expression:** Engage in activities that stimulate creativity and passion.

First Quarter:
The Time of Challenges, Making Decisions

The First Quarter, or Half Moon, occurs when the moon is half-illuminated, symbolising the need for balance and decision-making. This phase often brings challenges or obstacles that must be overcome to continue your path.

Rituals for the First Quarter

- **Embrace Challenge:** Identify and address obstacles or challenges. Use this energy to overcome difficulties and make necessary decisions.
- **Empowerment Practices:** Engage in practices that enhance your personal power and confidence.

WAXING GIBBOUS: THE PHASE OF REFINEMENT, PREPARATION

As the moon waxes full, it enters the Waxing Gibbous phase, appearing almost full. This is a time of intense and charged heightened energy. This calls for refinement and preparation. Your goals are nearing fruition of your efforts; this phase calls for careful review and adjustment. The energy is at its fullest. Waxing Gibbous is about being thorough and thoughtful, addressing any last-minute details, preparation for the outcome.

RITUALS FOR THE WAXING GIBBOUS
- **Refinement:** Review and fine-tune your plans or projects. Pay attention to details and make necessary adjustments.
- **Preparation for Completion:** Prepare for the culmination of your efforts. Visualise successful outcomes and embrace the energy of completion.

FULL MOON: TIME OF CULMINATION, ILLUMINATION, THE LUTEAL PHASE

The Full Moon is the pinnacle of the lunar cycle, when the moon is fully illuminated and at its brightest. This phase represents culmination, completion, and illumination. The menstrual cycle corresponds to the luteal phase, where the body either supports a potential pregnancy or begins preparing for menstruation. The Full Moon brings heightened emotions and insights, making it a powerful time for emotional healing, spiritual work, and rituals of release. Just as the luteal phase can bring about intense emotions and self-reflection, the Full Moon invites you to celebrate your achievements, gain clarity, and release what no longer serves you.

Rituals for the Full Moon

- **Release Ceremony:** Let go of what no longer serves you. Perform rituals to release emotional baggage, old habits, or limiting beliefs.
- **Celebration:** Acknowledge and celebrate your achievements and progress. Engage in practices that bring joy and fulfilment.

Waning Gibbous:
Phase of Gratitude, Sharing, the Late Luteal Phase

After the Full Moon, the Waning Gibbous phase begins as the moon wanes. This phase is characterised by a gentle decline in energy, prompting reflection and gratitude. It's a period for introspection and recognising the lessons learned during the lunar cycle, much like the introspection that often accompanies the premenstrual phase.

In the menstrual cycle, this phase corresponds to the late luteal phase, where energy may begin to wane and the body prepares for menstruation. The Waning Gibbous is a time to appreciate your accomplishments and share your knowledge, resources, or insights with others.

Rituals for the Waning Gibbous

- **Gratitude Practice:** Express gratitude for the lessons learned and the progress made. Share your insights with others.
- **Reflective Journaling:** Reflect on the past lunar cycle, noting what worked well and what needs adjustment.

LAST QUARTER: TIME OF REFLECTION, RELEASE

The Last Quarter, also known as the Third Quarter, occurs when the moon is once again half-illuminated, but now it is waning. This phase signals a time of re-evaluation, reflection, and release. The Last Quarter encourages you to let go of what no longer serves you outdated beliefs, toxic relationships, or unproductive habits. It's a time for emotional detox, cleansing practices, and release.

WANING CRESCENT: REST, RETREAT, CLOSURE

The Waning Crescent is the final phase of the lunar cycle, where the moon's light is almost entirely gone. This phase represents a period of rest, retreat, and closure. The Waning Crescent invites you to turn inward, recharge, and prepare for the next New Moon. It is a time for deep reflection, examining the past month's journey, and letting go of any remaining attachments. This phase encourages a focus on healing, regeneration, and inner peace, setting the stage for a fresh start with the upcoming New Moon and menstrual cycle.

LUNAR CYCLE

The moon remains a powerful guide for your inner journey, helping you connect with the natural rhythms of life. The moon's phases impact all life on Earth, serving as a potent tool for maintaining balance, harmony, and a connection with your inner self. The lunar cycle, with its regular phases, offers a structure for self-reflection, intention-setting, and spiritual growth. By aligning with the moon's energy, you tap into the cyclical nature of existence, using each phase to nurture your intentions, release what no longer serves you, and embrace the transformative power of the natural world.

RITUAL FOR ALIGNING WITH THE MOON'S ENERGY

- **Choose Your Phase:** Select a moon phase that resonates with your current life situation. For instance, if you seek to set new intentions, begin on the New Moon. On the evening of the chosen phase, find a quiet, comfortable space where you won't be disturbed. Light a candle to symbolise the moon's light, and close your eyes, taking a few deep breaths to centre yourself.
- **Reflection:** Hold a journal or piece of paper and reflect on the moon phase and its relevance to your life's current cycle. Write down your thoughts, intentions, or anything you wish to release. For the New Moon, write your intentions for the upcoming cycle. For the Full Moon, note what you want to celebrate or release.
- **Visualisation and Release:** Once you have finished writing, hold the paper close to your heart and visualise the moon's energy infusing your intentions with power and light. When you feel ready, safely burn the paper in a fireplace, fire bowl or metal container to symbolise the release of your intentions into the universe or keep it as a reminder of your commitment.
- **Closing:** Express gratitude to the moon and yourself for taking this time to align with the natural world. Extinguish the candle, knowing that the moon's energy will continue to guide and support you through the cycle.

New Moon Manifestation Ritual

The New Moon is a powerful time for setting intentions and manifesting changes, including restoring your menstrual cycle.

- **Create a Vision Board:** On the night of the new moon, create a vision board or journal entry focused on your intention to reconnect with your moon cycle. Include images, words, and symbols representing your desire for harmony and balance within your body. As you create, feel the energy of the new moon illuminating the path to your heart's desire.
- **Affirm and Release:** Once your intention is clear, release it to the universe by either burying the vision board in the Earth or safely burning it in a fire, knowing that the new moon's energies are carrying your desires. Feel the release as a moment of surrender, trusting that your desires are being woven into the cosmic tapestry.

Full Moon Gazing Ritual, Meditation, and Sacred Bath

Purpose: The Full Moon is a powerful time for culmination, illumination, and release. This ritual helps you connect with its potent energy, allowing you to reflect on your journey, celebrate achievements, and release what no longer serves you. Incorporating a sacred ritual bath can enhance your connection with the moon's energy, offering a cleansing and rejuvenating experience.

Preparation:
- Choose a location where you can clearly see the Full Moon, whether outdoors or near a window with a good view of the sky.

- Gather items that help you feel centred and grounded, such as a blanket, comfortable clothing, crystals (like moonstone or selenite), and a journal.
- Prepare your sacred ritual bath with candles, essential oils, sea salt, and herbs (like lavender or rosemary).
- Light a candle or incense to create a sacred space.

RITUAL STEPS

- **Create Your Sacred Space:** Begin by setting up your space with intention. Lay down your blanket or find a comfortable seat where you can relax and see the Full Moon. Light your candle or incense and place your crystals nearby if you have them. As you arrange your space, focus on creating a calm, peaceful environment where you can fully immerse yourself in the ritual. For a sacred bath, prepare your bath by filling it with warm water, adding sea salt, essential oils, and herbs. Let the bath water absorb your intentions as you prepare.
- **Grounding Meditation:** Sit comfortably with your spine straight and your hands resting gently on your knees. Close your eyes and take a few deep breaths, inhaling deeply through your nose and exhaling slowly through your mouth. Visualise roots extending from your body into the Earth, anchoring you securely to the ground. Feel the connection with the Earth, allowing it to stabilise and support you. Take a moment to set your intention for this ritual—to gain clarity, release old patterns, or simply connect more deeply with the moon's energy.
- **Full Moon Gazing:** Open your eyes and turn your gaze to the Full Moon. Take in its brightness and let its light fill your vision. Breathe deeply as you connect with the moon's energy, allowing it to wash over you. As you gaze at the

moon, reflect on the past month. Consider what you have accomplished, the challenges you've faced, and the lessons you've learned. Observe any thoughts or emotions that arise, letting them flow without judgment.

REFLECTION AND RELEASE

After moon gazing, write down your reflections in your journal. Consider these questions:

- What has come to fruition in my life?
- What am I ready to release?
- What no longer serves my highest good?

Write freely, allowing your thoughts and feelings to flow. When finished, review your reflections and identify what you wish to release under the Full Moon's light.

SACRED RITUAL BATH

After your reflections, transition into a sacred ritual bath to deepen your connection with the Full Moon's energy. Enter the bath slowly, feeling the warm water embrace you. As you soak, visualise the moon's light pouring into the water, cleansing your body, mind, and spirit. Allow the water to wash away any negativity, stress, or emotional burdens you carry. You may wish to speak aloud or silently affirm what you are releasing, letting the water absorb it and carry it away. Spend some time in quiet meditation, focusing on the renewal and clarity you are receiving from the Full Moon's energy. As you drain the bath, imagine all that you are releasing flowing away with the water.

Release Ritual:
After your sacred bath, return to your Full Moon gazing space. Hold your journal close to your heart and close your eyes again. Visualise the moon's light pouring into you, illuminating every part of your being. Imagine this light cleansing you of anything negative, outdated, or unnecessary. Speak aloud or silently declare what you wish to release. "Under the light of this Full Moon, I release [name what you wish to let go of]. I free myself from its hold and make space for new energy and opportunities."

Closing the Ritual:
After your release, take a few more deep breaths, feeling lighter and more open. If you are comfortable, you can safely burn the page of your journal with your release statements (using a fireproof dish) to symbolise letting go, or you can tear it up and dispose of it in a way that feels right to you. As you do this, thank the moon for its guidance and support.

Final Meditation:
To close, return to your meditative position and focus on your breath. Visualise yourself bathed in moonlight, renewed and filled with peace. Take a moment to express gratitude for the clarity and healing you've received. When you feel ready, slowly bring your awareness back to the present moment, gently opening your eyes.

Express Gratitude:
Extinguish your candle or incense as a symbolic gesture to close the ritual. Thank the moon, the Earth, and yourself for this time of reflection and connection. Know that the energy of the Full Moon will continue to support you as you move forward.

Post Ritual:
After your ritual, spend some time in quiet reflection or, if possible, take a gentle walk in the moonlight. Allow the energy of

the Full Moon to continue to work through you and consider integrating any insights you gained into your daily life. The sacred bath can leave you feeling deeply cleansed and rejuvenated, providing a sense of renewal as you move forward with the moon's cycle.

FULL MOON RITUAL:
HONOURING THE DIVINE FEMININE

The Full Moon is a time of completion, illumination, and heightened intuition. It is an ideal moment to honour the divine feminine and tap into the wisdom that lies within. This ritual will help you connect with the fullness of the lunar energy and celebrate the divine feminine in all its aspects.

Materials for Honouring the Divine Feminine:
- White candle
- Bowl of water
- Moonstone or other moon related crystals (selenite, clear quartz)
- Incense or Sage for cleansing
- Journal and Pen
- Flowers or other natural items that represent the feminine
- An altar space (can be a small table or a dedicated spot in your home).

RITUAL STEPS

- Prepare Your Space: Cleanse the space with incense or sage to remove any negative energy. Arrange your altar with a white candle, bowl of water, crystals, flowers, and any other items that resonate with the divine feminine.
- Grounding and Centring: Sit comfortably in front of your

altar. Take several deep breaths, inhaling through your nose and exhaling through your mouth. Visualise roots growing from the base of your spine and the soles of your feet, anchoring you deep into the Earth.
- Calling in the Four Directions: Face each cardinal direction and invite the energies of the elements to join your ritual:
    o East (Air): "I call upon the energies of the East, of Air and inspiration. May your wisdom and clarity guide this ritual."
    o South (Fire): "I call upon the energies of the South, of Fire and passion. May your strength and transformation empower this ritual."
    o West (Water): "I call upon the energies of the West, of Water and intuition. May your depth and emotion enrich this ritual."
    o North (Earth): "I call upon the energies of the North, of Earth and stability. May your grounding and support steady this ritual."
- Light the Candle: Light the white candle and say: "I light this candle to honour the Full Moon and the divine feminine. May her light illuminate my path and guide me to wisdom and understanding."
- Meditation and Reflection: Hold the moonstone or crystal in your hand. Close your eyes and meditate on the Full Moon's light, feeling its energy fill your being. Reflect on the aspects of the divine feminine you wish to honour: compassion, intuition, creativity, strength, and nurturing. Allow these qualities to resonate within you.
- Water Blessing: Dip your fingers into the bowl of water and sprinkle a few drops on yourself, saying: "I bless myself with the waters of the moon, cleansing and renewing my spirit."
- Journaling: Spend some time writing in your journal. Reflect on the past lunar cycle, noting any significant

experiences, insights, or lessons. Consider what has come to fruition and what you are ready to release.
- Closing the Ritual: Thank the energies of the four directions for their presence and guidance. Extinguish the candle, knowing that the energy remains with you. Say: "I give thanks to the divine feminine and the wisdom of the Full Moon. May her blessings continue to guide and protect me."

NEW MOON RITUAL: HONOURING THE DIVINE FEMININE

The New Moon is a time of new beginnings, setting intentions, and planting seeds for the future. Honouring the divine feminine and embracing her nurturing, creative energy is a powerful way to harness this potential. This ritual will help you connect with the possibilities of the lunar cycle and honour the divine feminine within.

Materials Needed:
- Black, purple or dark blue candle
- A small pot of soil and seeds (or a plant)
- Rose quartz or other related crystals (amethyst, labradorite)
- Incense or sage for cleansing
- Journal and pen
- Symbols of new beginnings (acorns, buds, eggs)
- An altar space

RITUAL STEPS

- **Prepare Your Space:** Cleanse the space with incense or sage to create a sacred environment. Arrange your altar

with the dark candle, pot of soil and seeds, crystals, and symbols of new beginnings. Focus on creating a space that feels peaceful and aligned with your intentions.
- **Grounding and Centring:** Sit comfortably in front of your altar. Take several deep breaths, inhaling through your nose and exhaling through your mouth. Visualise roots growing from the base of your spine and the soles of your feet, anchoring you deep into the Earth.
- **Calling in the Four Directions:** Face each cardinal direction and invite the energies of the elements to join your ritual:
- **East (Air):** "I call upon the energies of the East, of Air and new beginnings. May your inspiration and clarity guide this ritual."
- **South (Fire):** "I call upon the energies of the South, of Fire and passion. May your strength and transformation empower this ritual."
- **West (Water):** "I call upon the energies of the West, of Water and intuition. May your depth and emotion enrich this ritual."
- **North (Earth):** "I call upon the energies of the North, of Earth and stability. May your grounding and support steady this ritual."

FULL MOON RITUAL: CREATING SACRED MOON WATER

The Full Moon is a powerful time for harnessing energy, clarity, and intention. Creating Moon Water under the light of the Full Moon is a sacred practice that captures the moon's potent energy, imbuing the water with its essence. This water can be used for spiritual practices, cleansing, and enhancing rituals throughout the lunar cycle.

Materials Needed:
- A clear glass jar or bottle with a lid
- Fresh, pure water (preferably spring or filtered water)
- Crystals (clear quartz or moonstone are ideal)
- A white candle
- Sage, Palo Santo, or incense for cleansing
- A small cloth or covering for the jar
- A sacred space or altar
- Journal and Pen for reflection

RITUAL STEPS

Prepare Your Space: Begin by choosing a quiet, sacred space where you can clearly see the Full Moon. This could be outside in nature or near a window where the moonlight will touch your jar of water. Cleanse the space with sage, Palo Santo, or incense, allowing the smoke to purify the area and your materials.

- **Gather Your Materials:** Place the jar or bottle in your chosen space, along with any crystals you may wish to charge with the Moon Water. Light a white candle to symbolise the moon's light and to create a sacred atmosphere. If you're using a small cloth, keep it nearby to cover the jar later.
- **Set Your Intentions:** Hold the jar of water in your hands and take a few deep breaths to centre yourself. Close your eyes and connect with the energy of the Full Moon. Set a clear intention for the Moon Water. This could be for healing, protection, clarity, or any other purpose that aligns with your current needs. As you focus on your intention, visualise the water absorbing the moon's energy, becoming infused with your purpose.
- **Bless the Water:** Raise the jar towards the Full Moon and

speak a blessing over the water. You might say: "Under the light of this Full Moon, I bless this water with the moon's sacred energy. May it be filled with light, love, and the essence of divine wisdom. May it serve to heal, protect, and guide me on my journey. As I align with the lunar cycle, may this water reflect my highest intentions and carry the energy of the moon within it."

- **Place the Jar in Moonlight:** Place the jar or bottle in a spot where it will be bathed in the Full Moon's light. If you're outdoors, ensure it is in a safe, undisturbed location. If indoors, position it near a window where the moonlight will shine on it. Place the crystals around or inside the jar to amplify the energy.
- **Meditation:** While the jar is bathing in the moonlight, take a moment to meditate. Sit comfortably near the water, close your eyes, and focus on your breath. Visualise the moon's light filling the water with energy, glowing brightly within the jar.
- **Reflection:** Reflect on the intentions you've set and the qualities you wish to imbue into the water. Allow yourself to feel connected to the moon, the water, and the natural world.
- **Closing the Ritual:** After spending some time in meditation and reflection, gently cover the jar with the cloth if desired, symbolising protection and containment of the moon's energy. Leave the jar in the moonlight overnight to fully absorb the energy. Before going to bed, thank the moon for its guidance and energy, and extinguish the candle.
- **Collecting Your Moon Water:** The next morning, retrieve your jar of Moon Water before the sun rises or shortly thereafter. Hold the jar and take a moment to reconnect with the intention you set. You may wish to say a final

blessing or simply express gratitude for the energy contained within the water. Store your Moon Water in a sacred space, on your altar, or in a cool, dark place.

Moon Water in Ritual:
You Can Use It in Various Ways:

- **Anointing:** Use the Moon bathing water to anoint yourself, your tools, or your altar for purification and energy alignment.
- **Drinking:** Take small sips of Moon Water to internalise the moon's energy (only if your water source is safe for drinking).
- **Rituals:** Incorporate it into other rituals or spells that align with your Full Moon intentions.
- **Cleansing:** Use it to cleanse your crystals, sacred spaces, or home, enhancing the purity and energy of these areas.
- **Baths:** Add it to a bath for a cleansing, rejuvenating experience.
- **Journal Reflection:** After using your Moon Water, take time to reflect on the experience in your journal. Note any changes in your energy, feelings, or manifestations that occur after using the water. This practice will help you track the effectiveness of your intentions and deepen your connection with lunar energy.

Full Moon Ritual:
Releasing and Manifesting with Fire

The Full Moon is a time of culmination, illumination, and powerful energy. It's the perfect moment to release what no longer serves you and too manifest your desires using the transformative power of fire. This ritual combines the illuminating energy of the Full Moon with the cleansing and manifesting properties of fire, helping you let go of the old and make space for the new.

Materials Needed:
- A fireproof bowl or cauldron
- Matches or a lighter
- A candle (white or red)
- Sage, Palo Santo, or incense for cleansing
- Crystals (clear quartz, citrine, or carnelian)
- A journal and pen for reflection
- A sacred space or altar

RITUAL STEPS

- **Prepare Your Space:** Begin by creating a sacred space where you can perform the ritual without interruption. Cleanse the area with sage, Palo Santo, or incense, allowing the smoke to purify your surroundings, your tools, and your mind. Set up your fireproof bowl or cauldron, and place the candle, crystals, and other materials on your altar or in your chosen space.
- **Set Your Intentions for Release:** Sit quietly for a few moments, focusing on your breath to centre yourself. Reflect on what you wish to release habits, thoughts, relationships, or any burdens that are holding you back. As these come to mind, write each one on a separate piece of paper. Allow yourself to be honest and open, acknowledging what no longer serves your highest good.
- **Light the Candle:** Light the candle, symbolising the illumination and power of the Full Moon. As you do so, say: "Under the light of this Full Moon, I call upon the element of fire to assist me in releasing all that no longer

serves me. May these flames cleanse and transform my energy, making space for new blessings and opportunities."
- **Burn and Release:** One by one, take each piece of paper and hold it over the flame of the candle, allowing it to catch fire. As the paper burns, drop it into the fireproof bowl or cauldron. As you watch it burn, visualise the energy of what you are releasing being consumed by the fire, transformed into smoke and ash, and carried away. As each paper burns, say aloud (or in your mind): "I release [name what you are letting go of] into the fire. I let it go, and I free myself from its hold." Allow the fire to fully consume each piece of paper, symbolising the complete release of these burdens.
- **Set Your Manifesting Intentions:** Now that you have created space by releasing the old, turn your focus to what you wish to manifest in your life. Close your eyes and visualise your desires as clearly as possible. Feel the emotions associated with achieving these goals joy, peace, fulfilment. Write each intention or desire on a new piece of paper.
- **Charge Your Intentions with Fire:** Hold each piece of paper near the flame of the candle (but do not burn them). As you do, focus on the flame's energy infusing your intentions with the power of the Full Moon. Visualise your desires coming to life, growing stronger with the heat and light of the fire. Say aloud: "By the power of the Full Moon and the element of fire, I manifest [state your intention]. May it grow and flourish, aligned with the highest good." After charging your intentions, place them somewhere safe, such as under your pillow, on your altar, or in a special box, to keep the energy alive as the moon begins to wane.
- **Meditation and Reflection:** Sit quietly, close your eyes, and enter a state of meditation. Focus on the flames of the

candle, visualising them burning away any remaining negativity and lighting the path for your new intentions. Feel the energy of the Full Moon surrounding and empowering you.
- **Closing the Ritual:** When you feel the ritual is complete, thank the element of fire for its transformative power and the Full Moon for its illuminating energy. Extinguish the candle, knowing that the energy of your intentions will continue to grow and manifest.
- **Dispose of Ashes:** Once the ashes from the burned papers have cooled, take them outside and scatter them in the wind or bury them in the earth, symbolising the final release of the old and the return of this energy to the earth, transformed.
- **Gratitude and Integration:** Take some time to reflect in your journal on the experience, noting any emotions, insights, or shifts in energy that occurred during the ritual. Express gratitude for the release and for the new opportunities that are on their way. As you go about your days, stay mindful of the intentions you've set, acting where needed to help them manifest.

DARK MOON RITUAL:
EMBRACING THE VOID AND SEEDING NEW BEGINNINGS

Purpose: The Dark Moon is a time of introspection, stillness, and preparing for renewal. It's a potent moment to clear away old energies, reflect on the lessons of the past lunar cycle, and plant the seeds for new intentions. This ritual helps you embrace the void of the Dark Moon, honouring the space of potential before the New Moon's light returns.

Materials Needed:
- A black or dark blue candle
- A bowl of water (to symbolise the void and the potential of new life)
- Sage, Palo Santo, or incense for cleansing
- A small stone or crystal (black obsidian, or smoky quartz)
- A small piece of paper and a pen
- A journal for reflection
- A quiet, dark space or altar
- Soil and a seed for planting intentions

Ritual Steps

- **Prepare Your Space:** Create a sacred, darkened space where you can perform this ritual without disturbance. Turn off or dim any lights to embrace the darkness fully. Cleanse the space with sage, Palo Santo, or incense, allowing the smoke to purify your surroundings and your spirit.
- **Light the Candle:** Light the black or dark blue candle, representing the mysteries of the Dark Moon and the fertile void where new possibilities are born. As you light the candle, say: "In the quiet stillness of the Dark Moon, I honour the void from which all creation arises. I embrace the darkness, knowing it is the womb of new beginnings."
- **Reflection and Release:** Sit quietly with your eyes closed, holding the stone or crystal in your hand. Allow your mind to drift back over the past lunar cycle. Reflect on any lessons learned, patterns observed, or situations that no longer serve you. When you feel ready, write down anything you wish to release on the piece of paper. This could be limiting beliefs, unhealthy habits, or lingering emotions. Once you have written down your releases, hold the paper over the candle flame, carefully burning it. As the

paper burns, visualise the energy of what you are releasing being absorbed by the flame, transmuted into light, and disappearing into the void. Say: "I release what no longer serves me. I clear the space within, making room for new growth and possibilities."

- **Meditation with the Void:** Place the stone or crystal in the bowl of water, symbolising the void of the Dark Moon the space of pure potential. Sit comfortably, close your eyes, and focus on your breath. Allow yourself to sink into the stillness, embracing the quiet, dark energy of this lunar phase. Imagine yourself floating in the void, free from past burdens, open to whatever new seeds the universe is preparing for you. Spend some time in this meditative state, allowing the darkness to cradle you and hold space for your new beginnings.
- **Planting New Intentions:** After your meditation, consider what new intentions or goals you wish to manifest in the upcoming lunar cycle. These could be personal, spiritual, or professional desires. Write down your intentions in your journal, focusing on the feelings and outcomes you wish to cultivate. If you have chosen to plant a seed, hold it in your hand as you write your intentions, infusing it with your desires. When you are ready, plant the seed in the soil, either in a small pot or outside in the earth. As you cover the seed with soil, say: "I plant the seed of my intentions in the fertile void. As the moon begins to wax, may my desires take root, grow, and blossom in alignment with the highest good." If you are not using a physical seed, you can visualise planting the seed of your intention in your mind's eye, seeing it grow and flourish with the waxing moon.
- **Closing the Ritual:** Gently extinguish the candle, thanking the Dark Moon for its wisdom and the opportunity to reflect and renew. You may wish to keep the stone or crystal on

your altar or near your bed as a reminder of the power of the void and the new beginnings it holds.
- **Integration and Rest:** After the ritual, spend some time journaling about your experience, noting any insights or feelings that arose. Embrace the quiet energy of the Dark Moon by taking time for rest and self-care, allowing the seeds you've planted to begin their journey of growth. As the moon begins to wax, revisit your intentions regularly, nurturing them as you would a newly planted seed, and take small, meaningful actions towards their manifestation.

NEW MOON RITUAL: PLANTING SEEDS OF INTENTION

The New Moon is a time of renewal, introspection, and setting intentions for the upcoming lunar cycle. This ritual helps you align with the energy of the New Moon by planting the seeds of your desires and goals, both symbolically and literally, cultivating growth and manifestation.

Materials Needed:
- A small pot or container with soil or a garden space if available
- Seeds or a small plant, herbs like basil or lavender work well
- A black, purple, or dark blue candle
- Sage, Palo Santo, or incense for cleansing
- A journal and pen
- Crystals (black obsidian, labradorite, or amethyst)
- A quiet, sacred space or altar

RITUAL STEPS

- **Prepare Your Space:** Create a sacred space where you can perform the ritual without interruption. Cleanse the area with sage, Palo Santo, or incense, allowing the smoke to clear away any negative or stagnant energy. Arrange your materials on your altar or in your chosen space, placing the pot of soil, seeds, candle, and any crystals you're using.
- **Set Your Intentions:** Take a few deep breaths to centre yourself. Hold the seeds or small plant in your hands and close your eyes. Focus on what you wish to manifest in the upcoming lunar cycle. Consider what new beginnings you are ready to embrace, what goals you want to achieve, or what aspects of your life you want to nurture. As you hold these intentions in your mind, visualise them taking root and growing strong, just like the seeds you are about to plant.
- **Light the Candle:** Light the black or dark candle, symbolising the fertile void of the New Moon. This darkness is a space of infinite potential, where anything can be created. As you light the candle, say: "In the darkness of this New Moon, I plant the seeds of my intentions. May they grow strong and true, nurtured by my will and the energy of the universe."
- **Plant the Seeds:** Gently place the seeds into the soil, covering them lightly with earth. As you do this, speak your intentions aloud, infusing the act of planting with your desires. "I plant these seeds as a symbol of my intention to [state your goal or desire]. May they grow and flourish, bringing abundance and fulfilment into my life." If you're using a small plant, place it into the soil with care, pressing the earth around it gently.
- **Water the Seeds:** Using a small amount of water, gently

water the seeds or plant, saying: "Just as I nurture these seeds with water, I nurture my intentions with love, focus, and dedication. May they grow strong and manifest in their fullness."

- **Meditation and Reflection:** Sit quietly in front of your planted seeds or plant, close your eyes, and focus on your breath. Visualise your intentions growing and thriving, just as the seeds will. Imagine the roots growing deep into the earth, drawing up the energy they need to flourish. Spend a few moments in this meditative state, feeling connected to the earth, the New Moon, and the potential for new beginnings.
- **Journal Your Intentions:** After your meditation, take your journal and write down the intentions you have set. Reflect on why these goals are important to you and how you plan to nurture them over the coming weeks. Writing your intentions solidifies them in your consciousness and serves as a reminder of the commitments you have made to yourself.
- **Closing the Ritual:** When you feel ready, thank the New Moon for its energy and the opportunity for new beginnings. Extinguish the candle, knowing that the energy of the New Moon will continue to support the growth of your intentions.
- **Care for Your Seeds:** In the days and weeks following the ritual, care for your seeds or plant as a daily reminder of your intentions. Water them, give them sunlight, and watch them grow. As they flourish, so too will your intentions. Regularly check in with your journal to track your progress and reflect on any changes or growth in your life.
- **Gratitude and Reflection:** As the moon waxes and your seeds begin to sprout, take time to express gratitude for the growth you see, in the plant and in your life.

The moon is not a doctrine. She is a dance. She is the breath of intuition, the pulse of remembering. When we move with her, we move with life itself. She says: "You are not late. You are right on time. Your cycles are sacred. Your becoming is blessed." And we answer: "I remember. I receive. I rise."

Let her guide you.
Let her soften you.
Let her make you whole.

Chapter 23
Sacred Mandala Integration and Reflection

Reflecting on Your Journey

As you have journeyed through the pages of The Mandala of Wisdom, you have likely encountered insights, practices, and tools that have touched your soul and inspired transformation. Now, it is time to pause and reflect on all that you have learned, and to begin integrating these teachings into your everyday life. Integration is a key part of sacred living it is through living the teachings that true transformation occurs.

The following questions and exercises are designed to help you reflect on your experiences, bring clarity to your path, and deepen your connection to the wisdom you've gained.

Questions for Reflection

What aspects of your sacred living journey have resonated most with you?
Reflect on the chapters that have touched your heart and mind. What teachings or practices stood out to you? How have these insights impacted the way you live your life?

Which rituals, tools, or practices have you incorporated into

your daily life, and how have they influenced your spiritual journey?
Take a moment to journal about how you've started incorporating new practices, such as affirmations, rituals, or working with the cycles of the year. How have they changed your relationship with yourself and the world around you?

What challenges have you encountered as you've explored sacred living, and how can you move through them with grace?
Sacred living can sometimes feel like a challenging path, especially when it asks you to face your shadows or shift long-standing habits. Write about any obstacles or fears that have arisen and consider how you can embrace these challenges with love and understanding.

How has your connection to nature, the Divine, or the Sacred Feminine and Masculine deepened through your journey?
Reflect on your growing relationship with the sacred, whether through connecting to nature's cycles, honouring your body, or embodying the sacred feminine and masculine energies. How has this connection enriched your life?

In what ways can you expand your practice of sacred living moving forward?
Now that you've explored these teachings, consider how you will continue your journey. Are there new practices or teachings that you want to explore? What commitments will you make to continue living with sacred intention?

INTEGRATION EXERCISE: THE MANDALA OF YOUR LIFE

Create your own Mandala of Sacred Living. On a blank sheet of paper, draw a circle in the centre. Around the circle, write the themes or practices from the book that have been most meaningful to you. These could include things like rituals, affirmations, self-love, divine balance, connection with nature, or creativity.

Within the centre of the circle, write a word or phrase that sums up your sacred living path. This could be your personal intention, such as "Divine Alignment" or "Living in Harmony with Nature". Colour the mandala with symbols or patterns that reflect your journey and place it somewhere visible to remind you of the wisdom and practices you've integrated into your life.

CREATING SACRED CLOSURE

The journey of The Mandala of Wisdom is one of continual unfolding, but it is important to mark a moment of closure in order to honour the work you've done thus far and prepare for the next chapter of your life. This ritual will help you acknowledge and celebrate the transformation you have experienced, while also opening the space for new wisdom and growth to emerge.

CLOSING CEREMONY: THE CIRCLE OF WISDOM

Prepare Your Sacred Space:
- Light a candle or incense as a symbol of illumination.
- Gather some sacred objects or symbols that represent your spiritual journey. These could be crystals, a journal, a feather, or anything that holds meaning for you.
- Set an intention for the ceremony—this could be a prayer of gratitude for the teachings or an intention for the next

phase of your sacred living journey.

Reflection:
- Sit comfortably, close your eyes, and take a few deep breaths.
- Reflect on the wisdom and insights you've gathered through
- your exploration of sacred living.
- Think about the practices that have grounded you, the shifts that have occurred within you, and how you feel as you stand at this moment of transition.
- Say aloud (or in your heart), "I am grateful for the wisdom I have received, and I honour the journey I have walked. I welcome the new wisdom and transformation that is coming into my life."

Circle of Wisdom:
- Imagine yourself standing in the centre of a circle of light.
- The circle represents your sacred living journey and the divine wisdom that supports you.
- Visualise the light expanding outward, filling you with warmth, clarity, and power.
- As you stand in the centre of the circle, place your hands over your heart and silently affirm: "I am whole. I am aligned with my highest purpose. I walk in harmony with the sacred energies of the universe."

Offering and Gratitude:
- In gratitude, offer something symbolically to the journey this could be a piece of paper on which you've written your commitments, a small offering to nature, or a prayer for continued guidance.
- Sit in stillness for a few moments, acknowledging the profound growth you've experienced.

Closing the Circle:
- When you're ready, thank the Divine, your guides, and yourself for the wisdom and transformation you've received.
- Extinguish the candle (if lit) as a symbol of closing the space, knowing that the light of wisdom will continue to guide you in your daily life.

MOVING FORWARD WITH PURPOSE

As you continue to live the Mandala of Wisdom, remember that sacred living is an ongoing journey. Each day is an opportunity to reconnect with your highest self, with the Divine, and with the wisdom that is already within you. Trust the process, honour your path, and move forward with the intention to live fully in alignment with your soul's calling.

As you step forward on your sacred path, may you walk with confidence and grace. May the wisdom you have gathered illuminate your way. May you always trust in the guidance of your soul, and may you continue to live in alignment with the sacred energies that surround and support you.

You are whole.
You are divine.
You are the wisdom keeper of your own sacred life.

With deep gratitude and love, go forth and shine your light.

The Journey Continues Within

Though this book may come to a close, the mandala of your sacred life continues to unfold—petal by petal, breath by breath. Every moment offers a doorway back to your centre, to presence, to the living wisdom that pulses through all things. Let this work not be something you've simply read, but something you *become*. Let it shape your days, your choices, your prayers. And when the path feels uncertain, return to the circle. Return to the breath. Return to the Earth. The sacred is never far—it lives within you, always. You are not walking away from this mandala. You are walking ever deeper into it.

Final Blessing
A Closing for the Journey

May these words arrive in your heart like a soft whisper from the soul, at just the right moment, in just the right way.

May they awaken what is ancient within you, a truth you've always carried, a tenderness you had forgotten, a knowing that needs no proof.

May you walk forward not as someone who has merely read a book, but as one who has remembered a path, reclaimed a part of herself, and returned to the rhythm of her own becoming.

May your presence deepen.
May your courage expand.
May your heart remain open, even in the face of the unknown.

And above all, may you remember your life is sacred.

Your voice is needed.
Your soul is wise beyond measure.

This is not an ending.
It is a spiral, a return to the centre of your being.

A return to the sacred.
May these pages serve as a lantern for the dark nights,

A compass for the wild ones, and a mirror for the soul that longs to be seen.

Blessed be your remembering.
Blessed be your becoming.

And so it is.

Glossary of Sacred Terms
A Language of the Soul

Throughout these pages, you'll encounter words that carry ancient resonance terms rooted in yogic traditions, shamanic pathways, feminine mysteries, and personal gnosis. Some may feel familiar. Others may stir something unnamed within you. All have been chosen with care.

This glossary is not simply a list of definitions it is an invitation into deeper presence. Let each word be a doorway, a vibration, a seed of remembrance. Return here whenever you feel the call to pause, reconnect, or simply sit with the sacred.

Glossary Terms

Anointing
A sacred ritual of applying oils to the body as an act of consecration, self- love, and spiritual awakening. Anointing connects the physical and spiritual realms, often used to invoke divine presence and deepen self-awareness.

Archetype
A universal energy or symbolic pattern that lives within us and represents aspects of the human soul. Archetypes such as the Mystic, Priestess, or Visionary guide us on our spiritual journey, offering insight, reflection, and empowerment. This book works

with archetypes like the Yogini, Urban Priestess, Shamanic Medicine Woman, Luminary, and Visionary to illuminate paths of sacred living.

Authentic Self
The expression of one's true nature, free from societal conditioning or external expectations. Living as the authentic self means aligning with your soul purpose and embracing individuality while honouring the collective good.

Awakening
The process of becoming more attuned to one's higher self, soul purpose, and the interconnectedness of all life. Awakening is a gentle unfolding a spiral path that brings deeper presence, remembrance, and clarity to one's life.

Ceremony
A sacred act or experience that marks transition, healing, or devotion. Ceremonies may involve words, movement, silence, music, symbols, or offerings. They are moments where time slows and the veil thins allowing us to honour the thresholds of life.

Circle Keeper / Space Holder
One who holds sacred space with presence, steadiness, and open-heartedness. A Circle Keeper creates and protects containers where transformation can occur, where all voices are heard, and where the unseen is honoured with care and reverence.

Divine Embodiment
The practice of fully inhabiting your soul's truth through the body. It is the sacred act of living spiritual principles in tangible, everyday ways where the mystical becomes fully human and the divine moves through each breath and action.

Divine Feminine & Masculine
The sacred polarities that exist within each of us. The Divine Feminine is intuitive, nurturing, and receptive; the Divine Masculine is active, protective, and focused. True wholeness arises when these energies are honoured and brought into balance within.

Divine Flow
The natural current of life that carries us when we are aligned with soul and spirit. Living in divine flow means surrendering to the rhythm of the universe and trusting that we are always guided, even when the path is unclear.

Divine Essence
The The eternal spark of divinity that dwells within all beings. It is your soul's truth, untouched by fear, ego, or external story—a place of deep inner peace, radiant love, and infinite wisdom.

Embodied Wisdom
Wisdom that is lived through the body, rather than merely understood with the mind. It is gained through experience, integrated through practice, and expressed through how we move, speak, and serve in the world.

Energetic Imprint
The unique vibrational signature you carry, shaped by your thoughts, emotions, ancestral lineage, and soul memories. It is the unseen essence you leave behind and the silent song you radiate into the world.

Gratitude as Practice
A conscious way of seeing and being that centres appreciation for what is. Practising gratitude shifts our vibration, softens the heart, and opens us to the sacred beauty woven into all of life's moments.

Healing Practices
Intentional tools and modalities that restore balance and wellbeing such as breathwork, yoga, meditation, journaling, sound healing, or ritual. These practices bring harmony to the mind, body, spirit, and energy field.

Heart Centre
The inner sanctuary where love, compassion, and inner knowing reside. The heart centre is both a physical and spiritual space, a portal between soul and world, where sacred decisions and healing begin.

Inner Wisdom
The quiet, clear voice that comes from your soul. Inner wisdom is accessed through stillness, intuition, reflection, and connection to the Divine. It is the compass guiding your sacred path.

Initiation
A rite of passage into a new layer of spiritual awareness. Initiations can be joyful or challenging marked by inner or outer experiences that call you to step into a higher level of truth, responsibility, and presence.

Law of Attraction
The The principle that energy flows where attention goes. Like attracts like. This law reminds us that thoughts, emotions, and intentions shape our reality, and that alignment with truth draws in more of the same.

Living in Alignment
When your actions, choices, and thoughts reflect your soul's truth.

Living in alignment brings a sense of ease, flow, and resonance with the path you are meant to walk.

Living Light
The eternal light of the soul the essence of Spirit that flows through all things. Living light is the radiance of truth, the spark of the Divine, the luminosity that lives within you and all creation.

Living with Purpose
The sacred act of living in service to your soul's calling. It is not only about what you do, but how you show up with intention, integrity, and devotion to the greater good.

Mandala of Wisdom
A sacred symbol and inner map for awakening. The mandala represents the unfolding path of the soul, with each petal or layer offering insight into your spiritual journey. The centre is your connection to Source the still point of truth within.

Mindful Presence
The practice of arriving fully in the now. With breath, attention, and softness, mindful presence helps us witness each moment as sacred and see the Divine in all things.

Mystical Gnosis
A direct and personal knowing of spiritual truth. Gnosis arises from within through experience, intuition, dreams, or deep silence. It bypasses doctrine and awakens the soul's own remembrance.

Oracle Wisdom
Divine guidance accessed through intuition, symbolism, and sacred tools like oracle cards, dreams, or synchronicities. Oracle wisdom speaks to the heart, offering clarity, comfort, and soul messages.

Power of Now

The portal to peace, presence, and transformation. The now is the only true moment we have where life is lived, choices are made, and healing occurs.

Rite of the Womb

A sacred ceremony of remembrance and renewal for women. This rite helps release fear, trauma, and ancestral wounding held in the womb space and restores its power as a source of creation, wisdom, and love.

Rose Consciousness

A sacred path of awakening through the symbolism and energy of the rose. It embodies love, divine feminine wisdom, beauty, and the spiral path of soul remembrance. The rose unfolds gently, one petal at a time.

Sacred Balance

The harmony between body, mind, heart, and spirit. Sacred balance is cultivated through awareness, practices, and rhythms that honour both your human needs and your divine essence.

Sacred Circle

A space of equality, unity, and shared intention. In a sacred circle, all are seen, all are honoured, and all voices are welcome. It represents the spiral of life, the rhythm of the cosmos, and the web that connects us all.

Sacred Feminine

Mysteries Ancient teachings, symbols, and ceremonies that honour the wisdom of the feminine. They include initiations, cycles, moon rites, womb healing, and the deep remembrance of what has long been hidden or forgotten.

Sacred Geometry
The language of the universe expressed through shapes, numbers, and patterns. Sacred geometry like the spiral, mandala, or vesica piscis connects us to cosmic harmony and spiritual insight.

Sacred Intention
A conscious desire or vow aligned with your soul's truth. Setting sacred intention is a powerful act of creation it anchors your energy and invites the universe to co-create with you.

Sacred Living
A way of life rooted in reverence, presence, and devotion. Sacred living is not separate from everyday life it is the conscious weaving of spirit into the ordinary, so that all becomes extraordinary.

Sacred Rituals
Intentional actions that open space for healing, transformation, or communion with the divine. Rituals may include movement, sound, symbols, or prayer and are often connected to cycles, elements, or archetypes.

Sacred Space
A container physical or energetic where the sacred is honoured. Sacred space may be a room, a corner of your home, a place in nature, or the heart itself. It is where you come into presence with what is holy.

Sacred Trust
A deep knowing that you are held by Spirit, by the Earth, by your own soul. Sacred trust allows you to surrender with faith, walk

with courage, and open to grace.

Sacred Truth
The eternal truths that live beneath surface stories and illusion. Sacred truth arises from your soul and aligns with universal wisdom. It is felt, not forced. Remembered, not taught.

Sacred Wisdom
The intuitive and ancestral knowing that lives within. Sacred wisdom cannot be learned from books alone it is lived, revealed, and embodied through presence and practice.

Self-Discovery
The unfolding journey of meeting your true self. Through reflection, ritual, experience, and soul work, you return again and again to your essence.

Soul Purpose
Your sacred mission in this lifetime. Soul purpose is not always a role or career it is a way of being, a path of service, and an offering of your unique light to the world.

Spiral Path
The sacred, non linear journey of growth and return. The spiral path honours that we revisit themes, healings, and lessons from deeper and deeper layers, always circling inward toward truth and outward into expression.

Spiritual Alchemy
The process of inner transformation where wounds become wisdom and the shadow becomes light. It is the turning of lead into gold using spiritual tools, presence, and truth to transmute and evolve.

Spiritual Practice

Rituals, disciplines, and daily devotions that align you with your higher self and the divine. A spiritual practice may include breathwork, meditation, journaling, yoga, or silence it is whatever brings you home.

The Heart of the Rose

A metaphor for the inner sanctuary of the soul, where love, truth, and divine essence dwell. Like the centre of a blooming rose, it holds mystery, beauty, and the eternal flame of your sacred self.

The Rose Lineage

A mystical path rooted in the sacred feminine, honouring the wisdom of Mary Magdalene, Isis, Sophia, and the Divine Mother. It is a lineage of devotion, remembrance, and sacred service.

Threshold

A liminal space between who you were and who you are becoming. Thresholds call for presence, ritual, and courage. They are sacred moments of becoming.

The Womb as a Sacred Vessel

The womb, physical or energetic, is the centre of creation, transformation, and deep knowing. It is the gateway of life, the seat of feminine power, and a temple of wisdom.

Womb Wisdom

The deep inner knowing carried in the womb. Womb wisdom connects us to cycles, creativity, intuition, and ancestral memory. It is a wellspring of healing and sacred feminine intelligence.

Epilogue
The Spiral Continues

This is not an ending. It is a spiral, a return to the centre of your being. A return to the sacred.

What you have encountered through these pages is not a linear path, but a mandala, a sacred circle that continues to unfold.

You may revisit these teachings again and again, each time, you will meet yourself anew. The rituals will evolve. The seasons will shift. Your relationship to the sacred will deepen with every turn of the wheel.

Remember, the wisdom is not in the words alone, it is in the living practice. It is in your breath, your altar, your presence. It is in the way you choose to walk through the world.

Let your life become the ceremony.
Let your heart be the compass.
Let the spiral lead you home.
You are the temple.
You are the prayer.
You are the wisdom keeper.
And the spiral continues…

ACKNOWLEDGEMENTS

To those who have walked beside me — seen and unseen — thank you. Your presence, your prayers, and your quiet guidance echo through every page. This book was birthed from the circle, from the sacred, from you.

To the women in my circles, my students, clients, and fellow seekers — this book belongs to you, too. Every ritual, every story, every line of poetry was shaped by your courage, your questions, your becoming. You are the bones and breath of this mandala.

To the Yoginis, Wild Women, Sacred Seekers, and Mystics — to all who have sat in circle, walked the spiral path, joined me in pilgrimage, danced through the seasons, and shared silence, laughter, grief, and grace — thank you. Your devotion wove this work with soul. You are the living altar.

To my wider community — too many to name, but none forgotten — thank you for your trust, your encouragement, and your belief in this vision. Your light carried me.

To my beloved teachers, guides, and mentors — those who shared truth through presence, paradox, and sacred challenge — thank you for the initiations, both tender and fierce. Your wisdom hums through these pages like a steady drumbeat. To the luminous ones in the unseen realms — your essence lingers in the stillness between words, in the hush of ceremony, in the breath before the next step. You walk with us still. May this offering be a prayer returned.

To the Earth — thank you for your ancient teachings. For holding me in the roots of trees, the song of rivers, the turning face of the moon. You were my first teacher, and remain my truest compass.

To my family — thank you for your love, and for holding the space for me to dream, to deepen, and to create. Your grounding gave this book its roots.

To the ancestors of this land, and to those whose blood and memory live within me — thank you for whispering through the stones, the flame, and the waters. This mandala remembers you.

To the part of me who listened — who stayed, who dared to remember — thank you. This book is the fruit of your quiet fire.

To Carolyn Burdet, my editor — thank you for your clarity, grace, and steady devotion. Your presence refined the offering and allowed its essence to sing.

To you, dear reader — thank you for walking this path. For opening these pages with wonder and willingness. May what you find here stir something ancient and eternal within. And to the Divine Feminine in all her forms — Magdalene, Sophia, Gaia, Cosmic Mother — thank you. May this book ripple outward as a devotional prayer, a remembrance, and a return to the sacred.

ABOUT THE AUTHOR

Julia Anastasiou is a sacred circle keeper, ceremonialist, transformational coach, and modern mystic devoted to the path of ancient wisdom traditions. For over three decades, she has walked beside women as a guide, a mirror, and a sacred witness — holding space in transformational circles, leading soul-stirring retreats, and facilitating life-changing journeys that awaken the sacred in the everyday.

As the founder of *The Mystery School of the Mystic* and *The Path of the Rose*, Julia weaves together feminine wisdom, yogic and Celtic traditions, somatic soul coaching, the rose lineages, and nature-based spirituality. Her work is an offering to the reawakening of the sacred feminine — intuitive, embodied, cyclical, and deeply rooted in the rhythms of the Earth.

Her spiritual path has led her through the sacred lands of India, the rose-woven sanctuaries of Southern France, the mystical landscapes of the British Isles, and the ancient Earth temples of Peru. These pilgrimages live within her as embodied initiations — transmissions that infuse her teachings with depth, remembrance, and spiritual resonance.

Julia's coaching blends sacred mentorship with practical soul-guided support. She meets each woman where she is, while gently holding a vision for her highest becoming. Whether guiding clients through soulful entrepreneurship, healing emotional wounds, or reclaiming their voice and purpose, she brings unwavering presence, compassion, and spiritual devotion.

From her garden sanctuary in Greenwich, London — a place of beauty, stillness, and sacred gathering — Julia bridges the seen and unseen. Her life and work form a living mandala: an invitation into presence, a homecoming to the sacred, and a reclamation of the feminine mysteries that dwell within every woman's heart.

CONNECT WITH
JULIA ANASTASIOU

If this book has stirred something within you an awakening, a remembrance, a longing for deeper connection to the ancient wisdom, you are warmly invited to continue the journey.

Julia Anastasiou offers transformation coaching, sacred circles, online classes, retreats, and soul-led pilgrimages through her platform:

The Mystery School of the Mystic. Explore current and upcoming offerings at: www.juliaanastasiou.com

Join the Mailing List
Receive sacred transmissions, lunar musings, invitations to global gatherings, and early access to upcoming events:
www.juliaanastasiou.com

Listen to the Podcast
Awakening The Mystic Within

Follow along on Instagram
Poetic insights, ritual reminders & glimpses into sacred living:
@juliaanastasiou108

A Gift for You

As a companion to this book, you are invited to receive a downloadable guided meditation: *A Return to the Sacred*.
Access it www.juliaanastasiou.com/themandalaofwisdom

More to Come

This is only the beginning. More books are already blooming — woven from the rose path, sacred travels, and the living mysteries Julia continues to walk. Stay connected for updates and early invitations as each new offering is birthed.

Blessed Be ... May the sacred rise within you, always.

Printed in Dunstable, United Kingdom

68413781R00151